Taylor's Guides to Gardening

Roger Holmes, Editor

Frances Tenenbaum, Series Editor

HOUGHTON MIFFLIN COMPANY

Boston • New York   1997

Taylor's Guide to Ornamental Grasses

For information about permission to reproduce selections from
this book, write to Permissions, Houghton Mifflin Company,
215 Park Avenue South, New York, New York 10003.

For information about this and other Houghton Mifflin trade
and reference books and multimedia products, visit The
Bookstore at Houghton Mifflin on the World Wide Web at
http://www.hmco.com/trade/.

Taylor's Guide is a registered trademark of Houghton Mifflin
Company.

Library of Congress Cataloging-in-Publication Data
Taylor's guide to ornamental grasses / Roger Holmes, editor.
      p. cm. — (Taylor's guides to gardening)
   Includes index.
   ISBN 0-395-79761-6
   1. Ornamental grasses. I. Holmes, Roger. II. Series.
SB431.7.T39 1997
   635.9'64—dc20   96-38427

Printed in Hong Kong

DNP 10 9 8 7 6 5 4 3 2

Cover photograph © by Jerry Pavia

Contents

Contributors

Sally Roth selected the plants to include in this book and wrote the essays and plant descriptions in the encyclopedia. She contributed to *Taylor's Guide to Fruits and Berries* and has written extensively on gardening in books and magazine articles. She is a contributing editor to *Fine Gardening* magazine and writes a weekly nature column for the *Evansville Courier.* She has studied native grasses and grown ornamental grasses in Pennsylvania, Oregon, and at her current home in New Harmony, Indiana.

Roger Holmes edited this book, ably assisted by Sarah Disbrow. He was coeditor (with Rita Buchanan) of *Taylor's Master Guide to Gardening* and several other titles in the Taylor's Guide series. He lives in Lincoln, Nebraska.

Consultants

Pierre Bennerup provided advice on *Acorus, Carex, Juncus,* and *Koeleria,* among other genera in this book. He is the owner of Sunny Border Nurseries, Inc., in Kensington, Connecticut, wholesale suppliers of grasses and other plants. He is also the owner of Comstock, Ferre & Co., in Wethersfield, Connecticut, the oldest seed company in the United States.

Kurt Bluemel offered suggestions on the genera *Festuca* and *Miscanthus.* He is owner of Kurt Bluemel, Inc., in Baldwin, Maryland, a mail-order nursery specializing in ornamental grasses and companion perennials. Through his lectures and appearances, he has been a major influence in the increasing use of ornamental grasses in American gardens. He has also introduced several fine new cultivars.

Carmen R. Hardin reviewed information about native prairie grasses, including *Andropogon, Schizachyrium, Sporobolus,* and others. She is general manager of CRM Ecosystems, Inc., in Mt. Horeb, Wisconsin, a native seed and plant nursery for the Great Lakes region specializing in consultation, restoration, and management of native ecosystems including prairies, woodlands, and wetlands.

Norm Hooven offered comments on *Calamagrostis, Melica, Milium, Molinia,* and other genera. He and his wife, Phyllis, are owners of Limerock Ornamental Grasses, Inc., in Port Matilda, Pennsylvania, a mail-order nursery specializing in ornamental and native grasses, rushes, sedges, and companion perennials.

Wayne Pauly supplied information on using fire as a maintenance tool for prairie plantings. He is a naturalist for the Dane County Park Commission in Madison, Wisconsin, and author of *How to Manage Small Prairie Fires,* available for a small fee from the Dane County Park Commission, 4318 Robertson Road, Madison, WI 53714.

Mark Stromberg offered advice about the native western grasses in this book, including *Bouteloua, Deschampsia, Stipa,* and other genera, and he provided up-to-date cautions on exotic grasses that are or may be invasive in the West. His extensive association with grasses includes work for the Nature Conservancy in Wyoming, Colorado, and New Mexico, and for the National Audubon Society grassland sanctuary in southeastern Arizona. He is currently manager of the University of California at Berkeley's Hastings Reserve, an oak savanna in central coastal California, and is president of the California Native Grass Association.

Mark Trela consulted on *Equisetum, Erianthus, Thypha, Zea,* and other genera. He is vice president of Fragrant Farms in New Harmony, Indiana, overseeing 25 acres of organically grown flowers, grasses, and other plants for the cut-flower market and dried arrangements.

How to Use This Guide

Grasses are among the most versatile garden and landscape plants, at home with annuals, perennials, and shrubs in mixed beds and borders; planted as individual specimens; massed over large areas; or whispering in the breeze above a patio planter. Ornamental grasses are also relatively new to many gardeners, who will find here a useful introduction. More experienced readers will find here a handy and up-to-date source of information on dozens and dozens of grasses, many of which were unavailable a decade ago.

How This Guide Is Organized

Like many of the books in this series, this one contains essays and a large selection of plants shown on color plates and described in an encyclopedia.

The essays

Three essays present an overview of ornamental grasses. In the first, we introduce the grasses and their close relatives, sedges and rushes, and examine their characteristics and appeal. The second essay looks at how these qualities contribute to garden and landscape situations. Photos on pages 46–113 illustrate the concepts discussed in this essay.

The plants

Recent years have seen a tremendous increase in the range of ornamental grasses available to homeowners. In this book we present a large number (nearly 200) of these. Almost all offer handsome foliage, striking form, and attractive texture. Many produce eye-catching flowers (small individually but impressive in the aggregate) and/or seed heads, and most provide interest in at least two seasons. Local nurseries are responding to increased interest in ornamental grasses, but still stock only a few varieties; all the plants in the book are likely to be available from one or more of the mail-order suppliers listed in "Sources of Supply" at the end of the book.

Gallery of grasses

To help you choose individual plants, the photos in this section will give you a good idea of a plant's foliage, form, and other attractive qualities. A short comment on the plant's use or character accompanies each plate, along with the page on which you'll find its encyclopedia entry.

Encyclopedia of grasses

If you're intrigued by a plant mentioned in an essay, shown in the Gallery, or that you see in a friend's garden, consult this section. The encyclopedia contains descriptions of each plant shown in the color plates as well as a great many additional cultivars and related species. The listings are arranged alphabetically by genus. (If you don't know the botanical name, look up the species by common name in the index.)

Each genus is briefly described, followed by detailed descriptions of selected species and cultivars. These entries present the plant's desirable qualities (and sometimes problematic ones), provide suggestions for using it, and comment on how to grow it.

A Note on Hardiness Zones

Plants vary considerably in their ability to withstand cold temperatures. Those native to high-elevation northern regions, for instance, can survive bitter cold, many degrees below zero, while some tropical plants may die when touched by the slightest frost. In the early years of this century horticulturists began to correlate the cold hardiness of plants with gradients of temperature as plotted on a map. The zone map on pp. 288–289 is based on one recently revised by the USDA, which represents 10 temperature zones for North America. The zone ratings given for each plant indicate the lowest temperatures the plant can usually be expected to survive. A plant rated Zone 5, for instance, should survive minimum temperatures between -10 to -20°F.

When selecting plants, remember that hardiness zone ratings don't account for other important factors, such as heat and wind. These factors are mentioned in the plant descriptions; if you're in doubt about a plant's suitability for your location, ask a knowledgeable person at your local nursery.

Gardening with Grasses

Not so long ago, a patch of ribbon grass by the back door or a clump of Eulalia grass standing sentry in the front yard was about as decorative as grasses got on residential properties. For most homeowners, and many gardeners, grass was the stuff they mowed every week, and the only grass in the garden was the lawn clippings spread among annuals and perennials as mulch.

Today, grasses appear in every corner of the home landscape. From neat tuffets of sheep's fescue, as springy to the touch as a pad of steel wool, to towering plumes of giant Chinese silver grass rising above a dense column of lush leaves, there is a grass that will suit any need. In beds and borders, some jostle for attention as specimen plants while others provide a backdrop for showier neighbors. Grasses dapple a meadow planting with splashes of gold, sway invitingly on the edge of a pond, and secure the soil on a steep bank. In a pot, a spray of arching leaves graces a patio. Planted en masse, grasses are the equal of many shrub borders and can be as effective, and much quicker, in creating privacy as the densest hedge. In all these situations, grasses can offer something special — changing colors and forms, flowers, seed heads — in each season. And if that isn't recommendation enough, grasses are among the easiest plants to grow, adapting easily to a wide range of conditions in the home landscape, where they are untroubled by pests and diseases.

What Is an Ornamental Grass?

Almost any grass can be decorative in the right place, but the ones commonly considered ornamental have a special appeal of texture, form, and color.

Foliage is the key to that appeal. Grass leaves or blades come in wonderful variations, from flat or pleated, bent or rolled to straight-edged, wavy, or wiry. These pleasing shapes often play a role in the plant's survival. Rolled or folded leaves, for example, preserve moisture in dry climates, while broad leaves capture scarce sunlight in shady locations. The varied foliage produces equally impressive plant shapes, from neat and springy fuzzcuts to gracefully flowing manes. Tufted grasses are usually the shortest, with thin, dense, spiky leaves. Mounded grasses have a smooth, flowing outline, like a waterworn boulder, an effect produced by leaves bowing over to the ground. Taller than mounds, arching grasses curve gracefully downward like the spray of a fountain. Upright grasses have a strong vertical line, with the leaves either in a tight column or a more relaxed V shape.

Many grasses exhibit two shapes at once, or they may change shape as the leaves elongate or the plant begins to flower. Some arching grasses bend only a few inches at the top, the rest of the plant remaining staunchly upright. Mounded grasses may gain an upright aspect when punctuated by tall flower stems. And many taller grasses, like the gardeners who tend them, stand upright early in the season and bend over as they age.

For many gardeners, the glory of ornamental grasses is color. From brilliant reds and golds to quieter earth tones and infinite shades of green, grass foliage can dazzle or soothe the eye. Likewise, variegated leaves (striped or edged in color) can shimmer softly or pulse brilliantly. Unlike perennials, which usually fade into oblivion at the end of the season, grasses are often at their peak of color during dormancy, when foliage mellows to tawny golds and warm beiges. As dormancy deepens, leaves gradually bleach to shades of tan and platinum.

While grasses are prized for their foliage, many also flower dramatically. Individual flowers are tiny, but clustered together they can be spectacular. Some have long, silken flower clusters that often ripen to puffs; others have spiky clusters, or plumes that look like giant feather dusters. Depending on type, grasses may flower in spring or fall. (See the discussion of warm- and cool-season grasses later in this chapter.) The flowers often last for weeks before giving way to seed heads, which are distinctive in their own right. Long after birds or wind have dispersed the seeds, seed heads persist, usually pretty enough to leave standing through the winter.

Grasses for Garden and Landscape

Of the thousands of grasses and grasslike plants with distinct ornamental appeal, we have selected several hundred for this book based on their beauty and usefulness in the garden or landscape. Included are true grasses and bamboos, grasslike sedges and rushes, and a few other plants resembling grass in looks and landscape use. We've drawn the line at grasslike plants such as alliums and daylilies that are valued primarily for their bloom. Ornamental grasses are increasingly available at local nurseries, but the selection is still likely to be limited. Because of this, we've done our best to ensure that all the plants in this book can be purchased from mail-order suppliers. (Consult the listing in this book, or ask your nursery to order for you.)

True grasses and bamboos

The family of true grasses, Graminae (also called Poaceae), is a conglomerate of 700 genera and 7,000 species that includes pasture and meadow grasses, cereal grasses, forage and fodder grasses, even grass used as timber (bamboo), as well as horticultural grasses grown as ornamentals.

All true grasses are monocots, producing a single seed leaf and mature leaves with parallel veins. (Most other plants are dicots, which have two seed leaves.) The stems or culms of a grass plant are hollow, except in a few species, with solid joints, or nodes. Bamboos, which range from miniature potted specimens to 40-foot timber giants, have prominent stems. But stems of other grasses aren't always apparent. Many are visible only at flowering time, when the culms lengthen and emerge from the tuft of grass.

In addition to their beauty, leaves of true grasses have an unusual characteristic familiar to anyone who has to mow the lawn every week — they continue to grow after being cut. Most plants have their growth points near the tips of the leaves and branches. Grasses grow from special cells located near their attachment to the stem, a survival adaptation to millennia of grazing and fires. Grass leaves are so eye-catching that they invite touching as well. While some are a delight to stroke, with velvety leaves as soft as a baby's downy cheek, others hide an arsenal of defenses. A look under a strong hand lens at prairie cord grass, for example, will reveal fine, serrated edges that can rip your skin if you stroke the leaf in the wrong direction.

The minuscule flowers of grasses cluster together, arranged on a stem in a tight spike, held separately on the thin stems of a raceme, or fanned out on the branching stems of a panicle, as shown on the facing page. Lacking petals to attract bees and other pollinators, grass flowers are fertilized by grains of pollen carried on the wind. Shake a head of timothy grass in bloom and you'll set free a smokelike puff of pollen, a floating sneeze waiting to happen. Flowers are held within spikelets of overlapping bracts. A hairlike awn may extend from the tip of each bract, giving the seed head a bristly or hairy look (think of a head of wheat). Sometimes the awns are extremely long and catch the light like strands of silk. When the seed head shatters, the awns wind into tight coils, propelling the sharp-pointed seed into the soil. Some grasses are both prized and reviled for their long awns, which make the grass shimmer like silver but have the nasty habit of lodging in sweaters and socks, and in the ears, nose, throat, and feet of family dogs and cats.

Sedges and rushes

In the wild, rushes and sedges are among the first to colonize wet spots. In the garden, they are ideal for filling difficult spots in wet soil or in shade. These grasslike monocots from the family Cyperacea can be difficult to distinguish from true grasses at first glance, but a closer examination will reveal differences. Most plants in this family have three-angled stems, which accounts for the old catch phrase "sedges have edges." Though a few species of rushes and sedges have round stems like grasses, the inside of the stem is pithy rather than hollow.

Most sedges grow in arching or erect clumps, while most rushes are travelers, spreading by creeping roots. As with true grasses, habit and form vary by species. While nearly all sedges and rushes prefer wet or boggy soil, some also adapt to average garden conditions.

Making Choices

Until recently, gardeners had limited choices among grasses. Plants now popular and widely available, like Japanese blood grass, were virtually unknown only 10 years ago. Today the challenge isn't finding grasses to grow, it's choosing from among the many available. Before you introduce it into your garden, you'll want to know whether a grass is an annual or a perennial, whether it grows in a tight clump or spreads

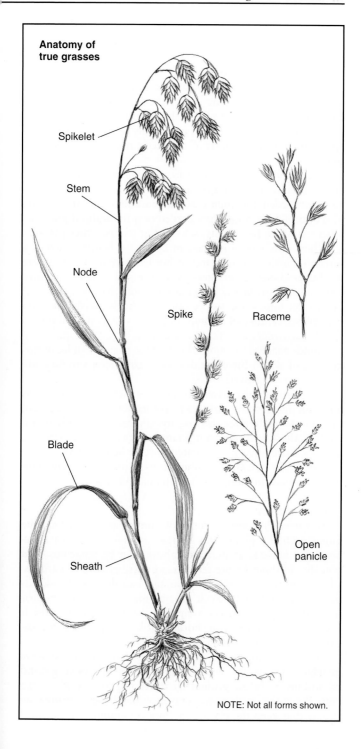

Anatomy of true grasses

Spikelet

Stem

Node

Blade

Sheath

Spike

Raceme

Open panicle

NOTE: Not all forms shown.

rapidly by runners, and whether it grows in the cool or warm seasons.

Annuals and perennials

Annual grasses sprout, flower, set seed, and die in a single year, while perennials are in for the long haul (some living for a hundred years or more). Though there are some biennial grasses too, they are not commonly available, even from specialty nurseries, and are therefore not included in this book.

You can sow annual grasses in a garden as you would flowering annuals. Their flowers and seed heads are showy in the summer garden and stunning in an autumn vase. Annuals are also appealing in a meadow garden or a naturalized planting, where they are free spirits, self-sowing among other plants.

Where you want a permanent landscape feature, such as a screen or hedge, or in a mixed border, perennial grasses are the better choice. Many grasses require you to take the word "permanent" to heart, growing enormous root systems that are all but impossible to pry out once they've settled in. You can still see century-old clumps of pampas grass so well rooted that homeowners who've inherited them have little option but to build gardens around them. The popular miscanthus grasses, of which there are dozens of cultivated varieties, are particularly long lived.

Some perennial grasses are less permanent. Pennisetums and blue fescues are sensitive to rot over the winter and can die out suddenly after thriving for several years. Others, including the lovely crimson fountain grass (*Pennisetum setaceum* 'Rubrum'), are not cold-hardy or heat-tolerant. These grasses might best be grown as annuals, just as we grow tender perennials like impatiens as annual flowers.

Root systems

You needn't consider roots of annual grasses, which die along with the plant after a single season. Roots of some perennial grasses, as indicated above, can be tenacious, and you should think before introducing these grasses to gardens. Chin-high prairie types, for example, can dig down twice as deep as their height. Such grasses may pose problems for neighboring plants by outcompeting them for scarce water. If you like to rearrange your borders or landscape, these grasses can also be a chore to move.

Even more important than the size of roots are the ways in which they travel. Running grasses spread above ground by stolons or below ground by rhizomes, rooting along the way. Bunching or clumping grasses expand their territory by shoots that keep the plant in a compact clump.

Be extremely wary of introducing running grasses into a garden bed. If you've ever weeded quack grass from among your favorite flowers, you know how difficult it is to remove the stubborn roots of running grasses. And don't be fooled by slow growth the first year. An old saying says, "The first year it sleeps, the second year it creeps, the third year it leaps." Because they root together to form a dense sod, running grasses are better used for lawns or extended ground covers. If you must have them in a border, confine them within deep vertical barriers or plant them in pots. Climate can affect the spread of invasive species. Running grasses are thirsty plants and their travels are curtailed where water is scarce.

Clumping grasses, on the other hand, make ideal ornamentals in garden beds or specimens in the landscape. The clumps expand slowly over the years, never taking over the border. Planted close together, clumping grasses may look like a solid stretch of running grass, but a close examination of the roots will reassure you that each plant is well defined and separated from its neighbor.

Warm- and cool-season grasses

Ranchers noticed long before gardeners that some grasses grow best in spring and fall, while others thrive in summer heat. These different schedules of photosynthesis evolved as a response to climate. Where summers are hot and bone-dry and winters mild, the native grasses go dormant, waiting for autumn rains before they green up again. Grasses like this are called cool-season grasses because they thrive in cool, moist weather, when the temperature hits about 65°F. They come alive in winter or early spring and flower from late winter to early summer, depending on species. After the seed ripens, they go dormant for the summer, sleeping until the seasons change again. Warm-season grasses, on the other hand, sprout up in spring, after the air and soil are warm. They flourish through the heat of summer, growing best when the thermometer climbs above 80°F. They flower in summer and fall. In fall or winter, they begin dormancy.

Most ornamental grasses are warm-season types. They grow lush throughout the summer, when the garden is at its peak, and offer a burst of late-season color and interest when they push up flowers. Warm-season grasses take on beautiful color for fall and winter, in shades of gold, tan, red, and even orange. As the plants sink deeper into dormancy, the foliage bleaches in the weather to hues of tan or straw and stiffens into its winter silhouette. Cool-season grasses are good for meadows or naturalistic plantings, and they offer early appeal in a border. In mild climates, their foliage is evergreen, at least over the winter season, and the leaves often take on hints of red and purple or yellow in cool weather. Some cool-season grasses bloom in spring but stay decorative in the garden for months. Feather reed grass *(Calamagrostis acutiflora* var. *stricta)*, for example, flowers in spring, but the golden spikes persist well into summer.

Transplanted from their natural, mild-winter climate to colder regions, cool-season grasses can behave like warm-season grasses, going dormant in the winter and waiting until spring to venture new growth. Summer dormancy can sometimes be staved off with regular watering, or by cutting back spent seed heads. Warm-season grasses can also produce surprises outside their natural setting. When the warm-season zoysia grass, which looks great in Florida and the Southeast, was transplanted to northern lawns, homeowners soon found that their green carpet turned brown at the first touch of cold weather — and stayed that way until late spring. Many of those zoysia plugs were pulled up and replanted with a more suitable grass.

Considerations of dormancy, foliage color, and flowering times aside, the warm or cool nature of a grass shouldn't affect its ability to survive in your garden. Warm- or cool-season grasses can be grown wherever they are cold-hardy, unless humidity or other extremes of climate are not to their liking (see encyclopedia listings for such cases). But keep in mind their seasonal nature. If your area is prone to long dry spells in summer, cool-season grasses will go naturally dormant, but actively growing warm-season grasses may need supplemental watering. If your winters are long and cold, your cool-season grasses may wait until the weather breaks before they begin to green up.

Sampling Grasses

Grasses have become so popular so quickly that a drive through town may be the simplest way to discover grasses that you'd like to have in your own garden. City dwellers can often find imaginative grass plantings along roadsides, in parks, at botanical gardens, or on the grounds of institutions or businesses. Repeat the trip every month or so to observe the transformations each season brings to the grasses you see. Washington, D.C., has many public gardens built around grasses, among them the work of landscape architects Wolfgang Oehme and James van Sweden, whose designs have been instrumental in the recent surge of interest in grasses. Some institutions, such as the Santa Barbara Botanic Garden and the Strybing Arboretum, both in California, include "wild" landscapes planted with native grasses and wildflowers. A visit to a prairie restoration in the Midwest offers the chance to experience something of the awe of early settlers who gazed upon an endless sea of grass.

Another way to immerse yourself in grass selections is a trip to a nursery that specializes in grasses, if you have the good fortune to live near one. (The resources section on page 290 includes addresses.) For those who don't, mail-order catalogs have the best grass offerings, but their simple lists, sparse descriptions, and limited photos can be a letdown if you're used to perennial catalogs. The best approach is to flag the grasses you like in this book, then search for the plants by botanical name in a catalog. Grasses are often known by more than one botanical name, so we've included alternate names in the encyclopedia entries to help in your catalog search.

Local nurseries won't have the breadth of selection of a good mail-order specialist, but more are including grasses in their demonstration plantings. Many local nurseries will be happy to special-order plants from wholesale distributors, and creating demand will bring more plants to local outlets where you can see the real thing before buying. If you order from your local nursery, be sure to supply them with the botanical name of the plant and any cultivar name, so you get what you expect.

Grasses in the Landscape

Striking foliage, clouds of blossom, glimmering highlights, music and motion — ornamental grasses are among the most rewarding and challenging landscape plants. Tall upright grasses make terrific specimen or accent plants in formal gardens. Arches or spills do the same for the casual garden. Low mounds and tight clumps are self-contained enough for rock gardens or edgings, and running grasses spread out for a soft effect as a ground cover.

Grasses also combine well with flowers, shrubs, and vines in borders, and they make excellent fast-growing screens, graceful buffers along the hard surfaces of walls and walks, and pretty potted plants. There are grasses for wet or boggy sites like water gardens and ponds, as well as for water-saving xeriscapes.

The wisest way to plan a landscape with grasses is to combine what you see and like in a grass with the knowledge of its general behavior and the requirements of your design. In this chapter we will discuss ways to use specific grasses in the landscape and offer suggestions for striking combinations with other plants.

Designing with Grasses

Before we look at specific landscaping situations, a few general comments about designing with grasses may be helpful. Grasses have distinctive silhouettes, often of striking size, that run the gamut in attitude from loose, floppy, and informal, to erect or compact and formal. Use these attitudes to impart or reinforce the character you desire for a planting. Be aware that site and companions can alter the feel of a plant. Set beside a doorstep or anchoring the end of a border, the tall, bare, flowering stems of the tall moor grass 'Skyracer' *(Molinia caerulea* ssp. *litoralis)* stand like a formal sentry. But dotted about a wild meadow design or set among perennials and succulents on a rocky hillside, clumps of 'Skyracer' blend right in.

Grasses grow fast, some approaching full size in a single season, and you can't prune or pinch them to keep them in bounds. So consider the mature size of the plant when placing it. Consider also its shape when in flower. In spring or fall (depending on the grass), flowering stems may suddenly rise well above the foliage, blocking the view of plants behind.

Designing with grasses, like all ornamental plants, requires consideration of foliage, color, and texture, and we'll discuss those qualities below. Most other plants, however, lack two of the most pleasing characteristics of grass: sound and motion. Grasses bow and dance in the breeze, each singing a characteristic song. Tall, wide-bladed grasses sigh deeply in a wind, while those with finer leaves sing a softer, higher note. As foliage dries and stiffens in dormancy, it emits a harsher, sharper rattle. Take advantage of this song and dance just as you do the fragrance and color of other plants.

Finally, when you design with grasses keep in mind that they don't fade into oblivion at the end of the growing season. Many gardeners think of fall as the best season for grasses. The warm golden tones set off colorful fall flowers and foliage beautifully. In colder climates, when fall turns to winter, grasses continue to add color and motion. Dormant grasses contrast handsomely with evergreen and berry-laden shrubs, while evergreen grasses, such as some bamboos and rushes, stand out in a sleeping landscape. Set against the pale leaves and soft plumes of a grass, the blackened seed pods of spent perennials form a lovely picture of contrasting line and color.

Grasses as Specimen and Accent Plants

Some grasses are so assertive in stature, shape, and color that they naturally create a focal point. Of all these qualities, height is the most impressive. Tall grasses make some of the best specimens simply because they're impossible to overlook. Giant cane *(Arundo donax)*, which reaches up to 25 feet, and cultivars of miscanthus and pampas grasses that reach 12 to 15 feet draw attention anywhere, especially when they're in bloom. A sense of proportion is needed when using these giants — they're too often seen towering precariously over much smaller perennials like Gulliver among the Lilliputians.

Some tall specimens have enough presence to stand alone, while others do better in a group. A single *Miscanthus sinensis* 'Cosmopolitan', with its broad, striped leaves, can anchor an entryway all by itself. But it may take three or five pampas grass plants *(Cortaderia selloana),* even with their towering feather-duster flowers, to set off a low ranch house. If you want to use a lanky grass such as giant cane as an accent, plant it as a screen or hedge at least 15 feet long to allow the plants to look architectural rather than awkward. To make a

Fine specimen grasses

Arundo donax (Giant reed)

Calamagrostis acutiflora 'Stricta'
  ('Stricta' feather reed grass)

Chasmanthium latifolium (Northern sea oats)

Erianthus ravennae (Ravenna grass)

Hakonechloa macra 'Aureola' (Golden hakonechloa)

Miscanthus floridulus (Giant Chinese silver grass)

Miscanthus sacchariflorus (Silver banner grass)

Miscanthus sinensis, all cultivars
  M. sinensis 'Strictus' (Porcupine grass)
  M. sinensis 'Variegatus' (Striped Eulalia grass)
  M. sinensis 'Zebrinus' (Zebra grass)

Molinia caerulea (Purple moor grass)

Panicum virgatum, species and cultivars (Switch grass)

Pennisetum macrostachyum 'Burgundy Giant'

Pennisetum alopecuroides (Australian fountain grass)

Pennisetum orientale (Oriental fountain grass)

Pennisetum setaceum (Crimson fountain grass)

Spodiopogon sibiricus

Interesting grasses for containers

Cymbopogon citratus (Lemon grass)
Cyperus spp. and cvs. (Papyrus)
Juncus spp. (Rushes)
Koeleria glauca (Large blue hair grass)
Helictotrichon sempervirens (Blue oat grass)
Pennisetum setaceum 'Rubrum' (Crimson fountain grass)

single specimen or a group stand out even more, plant it against a dark background or at the water's edge for high-lighting. The fine blades of 'Morning Light' miscanthus form a green fountain that contrasts with darker firs or spruces. When autumn comes and the grass mellows to the color of ripe wheat, the planting will light up like a sunburst.

Planted en masse, shorter grasses can make excellent focal points. All cultivars of switch grass *(Panicum virgatum)* are attention-getters in a mass planting, especially when they raise their airy, light-catching flowers. *Spodiopogon sibiricus*, with its leaves held at right angles to the stem, is another good candidate for mass planting. Shorter grasses make fine accents on a patio or along walks, walls, and fences. Pot them in containers or plant them in the ground along the edges. Line a walk with the delicate panicles of hairy melic grass *(Melica ciliata)* or plant ribbon grass (*Phalaris arundinacea* 'Picta') against a stone wall or around a flagstone patio. If it gets ragged, simply mow it down, water deeply, and let it regrow.

Grasses in Flower Beds and Borders

Gardening books are filled with time-tested combinations of annuals and perennials for the flower border, but designing a mixed border with grasses is relatively new. That leaves plenty of room to experiment. As newcomers to the border, grasses not only freshen a staid arrangement — a shimmer of fountain grass above lamb's-ears will show off the plant in a new way — they also improve a border's appearance in the off-season. The leftover seedpods and woody stems of perennials such as black-eyed Susan and purple coneflower are much more dramatic against the bleached leaves and soft seed plumes of grasses.

If you're adding ornamental grasses to an established bed or border, keep in mind that grasses are by nature thrifty plants, flourishing in soils that are lean in fertility and poor in texture. When they move into the loose, rich, deep soil of a prepared perennial bed or border, it's like switching from a futon to a featherbed. Too much of a good thing can make them weak and floppy. A leaner diet creates a stockier, shorter, more compact plant, which is usually what gardeners prefer. The grasses that do best in a rich bed are low or medium-high clumping grasses with a natural fountainlike habit. They'll maintain an attractive shape even if they get an energy boost from improved garden soil. Running grasses will take off through a collection of cherished perennials faster than you can say stop, and upright cultivars of tall grasses are likely to put on unusual height or fall apart. If you want to plant these tall grasses in your border, stake the tall ones up or plant them behind the prepared soil of the border proper.

In many ways, grasses are just like perennials when it comes to combinations for the border. There are choices that contrast dramatically with neighboring plants, those that complement other plants by showing off their color or shape to best effect, and some that echo their form, texture, or color. The following discussions cover some of the ways you can combine grasses and other perennials in the border.

Studied contrasts

The fine blades of most grasses look good against plants with large leaves, immense stature, or oversize flowers. If your taste tends to the extremes, try combining a tall grass of fine to medium texture, such as 'Sarabande' or 'Gracillimus' miscanthus, with the scallop-leaved plume poppy *(Macleaya cordata)*. The extravagantly large foliage of *Rodgersia* or *Rheum*, often difficult to work into the garden, can be gracefully melded with other perennials if it's brought down to size with neighboring grasses. Tall red swamp hibiscus *(Hibiscus coccineus)* is an inspired combination with a mound of *Miscanthus floridulus*, a substantial grass with strappy foliage. In summer, the lobed leaves and brilliant red hibiscus flowers shine against the green of the grass. In autumn, cupped seedpods stand out against bleached foliage and fluffy plumes. On a less extreme scale, hostas, bergenias, and other plants with good-sized, simple leaves also make fine companions for ornamental grasses.

Combining for color

Most grasses have colors that harmonize well. Their cool green or blue tones brighten the pinks, purples, or yellows of perennials, giving these colors more mileage in the garden. A few cheddar pinks *(Dianthus gratianopoltanus)*, for instance, interspersed in a spreading mat of springy blue fescue *(Festuca cinerea* 'Elijah's Blue' or other cultivars), have more impact than a solid planting of pinks.

Variegated grasses, with their cool whitened leaves, are beautiful with all kinds of border flowers. Variegated miscanthus (*Miscanthus sinensis* 'Variegatus') is perfect for the mixed perennial border, where its whitish green foliage provides a good foil for garden phlox and other perennials. And by the time the miscanthus flowers in early autumn, its rose pink panicles are a solo star in the border. The hot pink, salmon, and red flowers of coralbells (*Heuchera* spp.) show up vividly against ghostly white-green grasses, such as variegated bulbous oat grass (*Arrhenatherum elatius* var. *bulbosum* 'Variegatum'). Heucheras with deep-colored or fancy-leaved foliage, such as 'Palace Purple' and 'Pewter Veil', are standouts with plain green or gold-green grasses. Brilliant cerise phlox or any strong pink cultivar is made even more shocking when set against old-fashioned ribbon grass, and these garden phloxes can hold their own against the running grass.

Ornamental grasses can tame as well as brighten the colors around them. If you find your pink poppies have too much orange in them to look good next to the cool pink phlox, provide a visual interlude of restful green or gray-green grasses between them. The spiky leaves of small Japanese silver grass (*Miscanthus oligostachys)*, which stick out from the neat clump at almost right angles, make a good intermediary in the mixed border, adding lively texture but quiet color. A blue-gray-leaved cultivar of little bluestem (*Schizachyrium scoparium* 'The Blues') is another outstanding mid-height grass to settle into a mixed border.

Not all grasses mix easily. Those in the red range, with maroon or wine red leaves or hints of bright red, are a little trickier to combine with perennials. If the red tends to brown, try white or blue flowers with it; if it has a more purple undertone, go for pinks and purples as well. Grasses with yellow stripes, such as 'Goldfeder' miscanthus (*Miscanthus sinensis* 'Goldfeder'), have a warm tone that goes well with yellows and blues but clashes with most pinks. The cooler grasses with white-striped or white-edged leaves, like variegated bulbous oat grass (*Arrhenatherum elatius* var. *bulbosum* 'Variegatum') or variegated pampas grass (*Cortaderia selloana* 'Silver Comet'), make a good foil for pink, red, and white flowers, but are not so pleasing with yellow tones.

If you want to coordinate bloom times of grasses and perennials, remember that cool-season grasses bloom in the spring or early summer when the rest of the garden is also hitting its peak. By July, the show is over. Warm-season grasses burst into bloom in the fall. To be sure blooms will coincide, choose late-blooming flowers like asters or mums to accompany them. Remember to consider the height of flowering stems in relation to other plants in the border. Some grasses

Well-behaved grasses for the border

Achnatherum calamagrostis (Silver spike grass)
Agropyron magellanicum (Blue Magellan grass)
Briza media (Perennial quaking grass)
Carex buchananii (Leather-leaf sedge)
Carex comans (New Zealand hair sedge)
Carex plantaginea (Plantain-leaved sedge)
Festuca spp. and cvs. (Fescues)
Hakonechloa spp. and cvs. (Hakonechloa grass)
Helictotrichon sempervirens and cvs. (Blue oat grass)
Miscanthus floridulus (Giant Chinese silver grass)
Miscanthus sinensis, any cultivar, particularly:
   M. *sinensis* 'Strictus' (Porcupine grass)
   M. *sinensis* 'Variegatus' (Striped Eulalia grass)
   M. *sinensis* 'Zebrinus' (Zebra grass)
Molinia spp. and cvs. (Moor grass)
Muhlenbergia pubescens (Soft blue Mexican muhly)
Pennisetum alopecuroides 'Hameln'
   ('Hameln' fountain grass)
Pennisetum orientale (Oriental fountain grass)
Phalaris arundinacea 'Dwarf Garters'
   (Dwarf ribbon grass)
Phormium tenax (New Zealand flax)
Spodiopogon sibiricus (Frost grass)

Grasses to avoid in a border

These grasses spread aggressively by roots or stolons.
They can become a serious problem in the border:

Acorus gramineus and its cultivars (Japanese sweet flag)
Ammophila arenaria (European beach grass)
Arundinaria viridistrata (Running bamboo)
Buchloe dactyloides (Buffalo grass)
Elymus arenarius and cultivars (Blue Lyme grass)
Equisetum hyemale (Scouring rush)
Glyceria maxima and *G. m.* 'Variegata' (Manna grass)
Miscanthus sacchariflorus (Silver banner grass)
Panicum virgatum (Switch grass)
Phalaris arundinacea var. *picta* (Ribbon grass)
Spartina pectinata (Prairie cord grass)
Typha spp. (Cattails)

hold their foliage in a low clump but send up flowering stems that tower above it and obscure all their neighbors in the process — not a good choice for the front of the border unless the stems don't obscure the blooms behind them. Purple moor grass *(Molinia caerulea),* a low tuft with 4-foot flower stems, can stay up front because its stems are thin and widespread enough to allow a view through them.

Echoing effect

Grasses help to knit a landscape by repeating the form or color of other plants. An echoing effect is easy to produce in both foliage and flower. The loosely mounded hairy melic grass *(Melica ciliata)* looks beautiful beside old shrub roses, especially pink or red floribundas, because its arching spray of pale, whitish flowers mirrors the form of the rose bush. Golden hakonechloa grass *(Hakonechloa macra* 'Aureola') echoes the color of the gold-edged, bold-leaved hosta 'Aureo Marginata'. A more subtle echo can be had by combining a tuft of blue oat grass *(Helictotrichon sempervirens)* or blue fescue *(Festuca glauca)* with the scalloped leaves and nodding blossoms of blue Rocky Mountain columbine. Blue fescue adds texture to any plant with blue-gray leaves.Try it with the gray-blue foliage of cottage pinks and other dianthus, or with steel blue eryngium. For a combination of greens, try a green-flowered zinnia called 'Envy' against the spiky, pale blades of green and white dwarf ribbon grass *(Phalaris arundinacea* 'Dwarf Garters'), a more restrained cultivar of the typical running grass.

Tall grass partners

Perennials of great height usually hail from a prairie heritage, so it's no wonder their looks are improved when they're partnered with grasses. Clusters of madder-purple ironweed *(Vernonia* spp.), golden spikes of compass plant *(Silphium laciniatum),* and the graceful stems of prairie coneflower *(Ratibida* spp.) are right at home with big bluestem *(Andropogon gerardii)* and switch grass *(Panicum virgatum),* two grasses that grew with them for eons in the tallgrass prairie. You can translate the effect into other tall plant combinations, too. Try the satiny blooms of red or "black" hollyhock *(Alcea rosea)* with the vivid foliage of red switch grass *(Panicum virgatum* 'Rotstrahlbusch'), for instance.

Grasses with annuals

Annual flowers also look great with grasses. Orange California poppies and meadow grasses like *Stipa* are a natural combination that looks just as good in the garden as in the foothills. Or try russet-colored sunflower 'Autumn Beauty' or the shorter 'Music Box' *(Helianthus annuus)* with tall or mid-height ornamental grasses like sideoats grama *(Bouteloua curtipendula)*, switch grass *(Panicum virgatum)*, or little bluestem *(Schizachyrium scoparium)*.

Annual grasses are in turn excellent with annual flowers or perennials in an informal garden. They add a relaxed look, and because many of them are enthusiastic self-sowers, a meadowlike feel. For the same reasons, you may want to avoid introducing them to a formal perennial border. Hare's tail *(Lagurus ovatus)*, with its fuzzy tufts, adds lighthearted texture to an edging of dwarf or peppermint-striped zinnias. Tall annual grasses with large leaves and architectural form, like ornamental corn varieties, beg for equally outstanding partners such as tall, plumy celosia or the annual amaranth called love-lies-bleeding, which drips with chenille-textured pink flowers.

Grasses with Shrubs

All grasses combine beautifully with deciduous and evergreen shrubs and shrublike plants. Their fine texture against the stouter leaves and branching form of shrubs is always appealing, but never more so than in autumn and winter. The blazing scarlet of sumacs or the crimson-pink of a burning bush is amplified by a nearby planting of frost grass *(Spodiopogon sibiricus)*, whose leaves take on burnished tints of their own in autumn. Later, the spiky texture of the grass shows off against the shrub's bare silhouette. Evergreens reverse the spectacle. In winter they shine against the soft texture and pale color of dormant grasses.

Both clumping and running grasses can be paired with shrubs. Running grasses, such as blue Lyme grass *(Elymus arenarius)*, or self-sowing grasses, such as squirreltail *(Hordeum jubatum)*, can be set free to wander at will among large shrub plantings. With clumping grasses, allow several feet between shrubs and grass plants so they won't have to compete with each other for water and nutrients.

The design considerations discussed previously for combining perennials and grasses can apply to shrubs. Good combinations include contrasting, complementary, or echoing effects. It makes sense to vary the height of a planting, so that tall shrubs are partnered with shorter grasses and vice versa, and to avoid transitions that are too sharp. An extremely tall pampas grass may look awkward with a dwarf azalea. If you'd like to pair the two, adding a third, mid-height plant such as a pennisetum grass or a mugo pine will help make the jump. Low-growing shrubs like heaths and junipers work with mid-height grasses or grasses that grow in mats.

Shrub and grass combinations

Almost any ornamental shrub can be paired with a grass. Here are some good matches:

- Azaleas (*Rhododendron* spp.) with blue fescues *(Festuca glauca)* or plantain-leaved sedge *(Carex plantaginea)*

- Blue spirea *(Caryopteris incana)* with 'Blaze' little bluestem (*Schizachyrium scoparium* 'Blaze')

- Chaste tree *(Vitex agnus-castae)* with porcupine grass (*Miscanthus sinensis* var. *strictus*)

- Deciduous holly *(Ilex verticillata)* with fountain grass (*Pennisetum* spp.) and miscanthus (*Miscanthus* spp.)

- Japanese maples *(Acer palmatum)* with New Zealand hair sedge *(Carex comans)* or other sedges, or beside water with any rushes *(Juncus* spp.)

- Red or golden barberry (*Berberis* spp.) with blue oat grass *(Helictotrichon sempervirens),* blue Lyme grass *(Elymus arenarius),* or blue fescues *(Festuca glauca)*

- Red-twig dogwood *(Cornus stolonifera)* with frost grass *(Spodiopogon sibiricus)*

- Russian sage *(Perovskia atriplicifolia)* or butterfly bush *(Buddleia davidii)* with big bluestem *(Andropogon gerardii)*

- Smoke tree *(Cotinus coggyria)* with 'Yaku Jima' miscanthus, or with 'Sioux Blue' Indian grass (*Sorghastrum nutans* 'Sioux Blue')

- Star magnolia *(Magnolia stellata)* with New Zealand hair sedge *(Carex comans)* or with black-flowered fountain grass (*Pennisetum alopecuroides* 'Moudry')

- Sumacs, especially shining sumac *(Rhus copallina),* with purple top *(Tridens flavus)* or Stipa grasses or little bluestem (*Schizachyrium scoparium*)

- White-stem raspberry *(Rubus cockburnianus)* with Japanese blood grass (*Imperata cylindrica* 'Red Baron') and 'Flamingo' or 'Burgundy Giant' miscanthus

- Witch hazel (*Hamamelis* spp.) with silver banner grass *(Miscanthus sacchariflorus)*

- Yellow-stem dogwood *(Cornus alba)* with perennial quaking grass *(Briza media)*

Grasses in the Shade Garden

Most grasses are sun lovers, so it is surprising that some of the most beautiful ornamentals are at home in the shade. What they lack in size and showy bloom they make up for in stunning form. Colors are generally muted, with plants woven together in a tapestry of greens. Consider the foliage of nearby plants, and then find a texture and color combination that suits your eye.

The most elegant of all grasses, golden hakonechloa (*Hakonechloa macra* 'Aureole') is an exceptional shade grass, offering striking color as well as form. Developed from a forest grass of Japan, it forms a shaggy mound that weeps onto paths and over stones like a narrow-leaved bamboo. Its mane of golden leaves is beautiful with hostas, heucheras, and yellow Welsh poppies *(Meconopsis cambrica)*, as well as spring wildflowers and small bulbs. Vivid chartreuse leaves begin emerging about the time that hellebores and brilliant blue Siberian squill *(Scilla sibirica)* and glory-of-the-snow (*Chionodoxa* spp.) come into bloom. For a flourish in autumn, hakonechloa becomes suffused with pink before it dies back for winter.

Another beauty is the ethereal *Deschampsia*, or hair grass, which grows in the wild in lightly wooded areas. Both crinkled hair grass *(D. flexuosa)* and tufted hair grass *(D. caespitosa)* will thrive in light to medium shade in the garden. Tufted hair grass is one of the first ornamental grasses to bloom, and

Grasses for shade

Carex spp. (Sedges)
Chasmanthium latifolium (Wild oats)
Deschampsia caespitosa (Hair grass)
Hakonechloa macra and *H. m.* 'Aureola' (Hakonechloa)
Hystrix patula (Bottlebrush grass)
Imperata cylindrica 'Red Baron' (Japanese blood grass)
Luzula nivea 'Snowbird' ('Snowbird' snowy wood rush)
Milium effusum 'Aureum' (Golden wood millet)
Panicum clandestinum (Deer tongue grass)
Sasa palmata (Running bamboo)
Sasa veitchii (Silver-edge bamboo)
Sorghastrum nutans (Indian grass)
Spodiopogon sibericus (Frost grass)
Tridens flavus (Purple top)

its cloud of delicate panicles almost glows in the company of ferns and hostas.

The interesting grass known as bottlebrush *(Hystrix patula)* is a woodsy annual with bristly seed heads that look just like a slender bottlebrush. This grass is a good one to start in a naturalistic woodland garden, where it can self-sow with small black-eyed Susan *(Rudbeckia triloba),* blue American bell-flower *(Campanula americana),* and other shade-loving, summer-blooming wildflowers. No matter where you first plant it, bottlebrush will tend to gravitate to a place of honor along paths and openings where the panicles can catch the light. Children can't resist stroking its fully mature seed heads just to watch how easily they shatter.

Screening with Grass

When you want to hide a view of the street, your neighbor's RV, or the compost pile, you can install tall ornamental grasses for a fast-growing screen. Miscanthus and pampas grasses are popular choices for a screen, thanks to their great height and dense foliage. These grasses will give you good coverage in as little as two years from container-grown plants. You can mix and match for an informal screen, plant a single cultivar for a more conservative look, or intersperse variegated cultivars among green grasses for something different. Even a single plant of the variegated pampas grass known as 'Silver Comet' *(Cortaderia selloana* 'Silver Comet') will add interest to a plain green hedge.

An impenetrable hedge can be made of prairie cord grass *(Spartina pectinata).* Reaching 6 feet high, it has unfriendly razor-sharp leaf edges that discourage all who try to cross its

---

Grasses for screening

Arundo donax (Giant reed)

Bambusa oldhamii (Giant timber bamboo)

Calamagrostis acutiflora (Feather reed grass)

Cortaderia selloana (Pampas grass)

Erianthus ravennae (Ravenna grass)

Miscanthus, tall cultivars

Panicum virgatum, tall cultivars (Switch grass)

Phyllostachys aureosulcata (Yellow groove bamboo)

Phyllostachys nigra (Black bamboo)

Pleioblastus viridistratus (Golden bamboo)

Semiarundinaria murielae (Running bamboo)

path. You'll be able to block traffic from short-cutters or straying pets and enjoy rich yellow color in fall. Consider carefully before you plant — cord grass can spread aggressively, and it's no fun to try to remove. Corral the spread by installing a foot-deep barrier of plastic or galvanized metal at planting time, and be alert for escapees, which are easier to root out when young.

For year-round screening, turn to bamboo. Other grasses will have to be cut down in spring to allow room for new growth, so you'll be without a screen until the grass reaches full height in summer. Some hardy bamboos may shed their leaves in winter, but the stems will still have a screening effect. Yellow groove bamboo *(Phyllostachys aureosulcata)* and other semievergreen types hang on to their foliage through much of the winter. Black bamboo *(Phyllostachys nigra)*, with its unique glossy black stems, makes a spectacular screen, or a gorgeous addition to a screen of mixed grasses. Like yellow-groove and black bamboo, many bamboos are determined ramblers, and new shoots can spring up yards away from the parent plant. Don't plant them unless you have lots of space to sacrifice or you can install a deep, impenetrable barrier at planting time.

Ground Covers

Ornamental grasses, like their turf-grass cousins, make superb ground covers. Whether short or tall, clump-forming or running, any grass that spreads well can be an effective cover. The old favorite known as ribbon grass or gardener's garters *(Phalaris arundinacea* var. *picta)*, as well as tufted hair grass *(Deschampsia caespitosa)* and the beautiful blue Lyme grass

Grasses as ground covers

Carex plantaginea (Plantain-leaved sedge)
Carex texensis (Catlin sedge)
Deschampsia caespitosa (Tufted hair grass)
Elymus arenarius (Blue Lyme grass)
Festuca amethystina (Sheep's fescue)
Festuca glauca, species and cultivars (Blue fescue)
Koelreria macrantha (June grass)
Miscanthus sacchariflorus (Silver banner grass)
Phalaris arundinacea var. *picta* (Ribbon grass)
Sasa palmata (Running bamboo)
Sasa veitchii (Silver-edge bamboo)

(Elymus arenarius), are good mid-height ground covers. They combine well with ground-hugging junipers and heathers, or with red-berried cotoneaster. In a shady garden, clumps of plantain-leaved sedge *(Carex plantaginea)* provide a handsome ground cover.

Tall grasses and bamboos can also be used as ground covers, making an appealing grove of rustling foliage. *Sasa palmata* is a little tall for what we usually think of as a ground cover, reaching 6 feet or more in height, but it spreads rapidly by underground runners and fills in fast in shade or sun. This attractive bamboo has solid green leaves that spread wide like an open palm. Similar in shape but not in color are the striking white-edged leaves of *Sasa veitchii*, a smaller running bamboo that lights up shady spots.

If you're tired of mowing, consider substituting a naturally low-growing grass in parts of your lawn. Buffalo grass *(Buchloe dactyloides)* spreads by runners to create a thick, low turf. Several cultivars have been developed for western states because of their lawn-grass potential. One drawback is that the spiny seed husks can cling to pets and socks. Blue grama *(Bouteloua gracilis)*, another naturally low-growing species, is also getting attention as a low-maintenance lawn grass in the dry West.

A steep slope planted with ornamental grasses is much easier to care for and much more pleasing to the eye than one covered with turf grass. Both clumping and running types make excellent covers for slopes because their fibrous roots knit together to secure the soil. Running grasses will spread naturally to cover the area, but you can create the same effect by planting clumping grasses tightly together. June grass *(Koelreria macrantha)* is good for dry slopes.

A single mass planting of pennisetum is lovely on slopes, their arched foliage giving the impression of a waterfall. Mixed plantings provide more interest. The filmy white plumes of the spreading *Miscanthus sacchariflorus* make a striking early autumn combination with the warm chestnut-orange of little bluestem and the tawny gold of switch grass. For a low-maintenance slope that looks good all year, combine warm-season and cool-season grasses. The latter will be greening up as the former die down. Mixing warm-season grasses with evergreens, such as ground-cover junipers or heathers and heaths, will also add contrasting color and texture through all the seasons.

Meadow, Prairie, and Wildlife Plantings

Grasses are right where they belong in meadows and prairies. In spring and summer, native grasses are the canvas for the

Grasses for a naturalistic planting

Andropogon gerardii (Big bluestem)
Aristidia purpurea (Purple three-awn)
Bouteloua spp. (Grama grasses)
Eragrostis spectabilis (Purple love grass)
Erianthus ravennae (Ravenna grass)
Hordeum jubatum (Squirreltail grass)
Muhlenbergia filipes (Purple muhly)
Panicum virgatum (Switch grass)
Schizachyrium scoparium (Little bluestem)
Sorghastrum nutans (Indian grass)
Sporobolus heterolepsis (Prairie dropseed)
Stipa spp.
Tridens flavus (Purple top)

bright strokes of wildflower color, and when the flower show is over, grasses keep our attention with ripening seed heads and bright winter foliage. The plants on the list of grasses for naturalistic plantings are wilder-looking selections than the clumps recommended for accents or eye-catchers elsewhere. They'll offer good cover, a banquet of food, and a source of nesting material for birds, small mammals, and a host of other wild creatures.

Water Gardens and Wet Sites

A reflection in still water doubles the pleasure of a grass planting. Giant cane *(Arundo donax)* may seem out of place in the middle of a front lawn but is perfectly at ease at the edge of a large pool, its strongly vertical foliage providing pleasing contrast to the rounded leaves of other water plants, like lotus, lilies, and blue-flowered pickerelweed. *Miscanthus sinensis* cultivars are popular choices for the edges of smaller pools, creating rippling fountains of greenery that echo the ebb and flow of water. Mounded grasses such as fountain grass (*Pennisetum* spp.) and leather-leaf sedge *(Carex buchananii)* trail their leaf tips on the liquid surface of ponds, blurring the boundary between land and water. Upright grasses such as 'Karl Foerster' feather reed grass (*Calamagrostis acutiflora* 'Karl Foerster') add a formal touch to small pools edged in stone.

Grasses grown at the edge of man-made ponds don't necessarily find themselves in wet soil, but some grasses don't mind getting their feet wet and are good candidates for poorly

Grasses for water gardens and wet sites

Grasses that will grow in average garden conditions
as well as wet or boggy soil are indicated by an asterisk.
All others will grow in boggy soil or standing shallow
water.

Acorus spp. (Sweet flag)

  Calamagrostis acutiflora (Feather reed grass)

  Cyperus spp. (Papyrus)

Equisetum spp. (Horsetail)

  Eriophorum latifolium (Cotton grass)

Glyceria spp. (Manna grass)

  Juncus, all spp. and cultivars (Rushes)

  Schoenplectus lacustris ssp. *tabernaemontani*
    'Zebrinus' (Banded bulrush)

  Scirpus cernuus (Low bulrush)

Spartina pectinata (Prairie cord grass)

  Typha spp. (Cattails)

drained sites. Variegated manna grass (*Glyceria maxima* 'Variegata') will spread from dry land right out into the water. Feather reed grass *(Calamagrostis acutiflora)* adapts well to life in the muck. If you bring cattails (*Typha* spp.) into the water garden you'll admire their good vertical line and get a close look at the fascinating life cycle of their flowers. You may also get to see songbirds collecting the cattail fluff to line a cozy nest. Horsetails and rushes are other grasslike plants for water gardens and wet sites.

One of the most charming grasses for a wet site is cotton grass *(Eriophorum latifolium),* which sprouts furry white puffs in bloom, as if someone scattered a bag of cotton balls in the garden. This grass will grow right in water and looks great backed by purple or blue Japanese iris. Razor-sharp cord grass *(Spartina pectinata)* will flourish in a wet spot, but be sure to plant it well away from walks or swingsets.

A wet site can be home to a fabulous array of rushes (*Juncus* spp.). Soft rush *(Juncus effusus)* will sometimes show up on its own, brought in by birds' feet or sprouted from long-dormant seed. Its soft brown flowers dangle from the tips of the stems in an outward-arching burst of slim, dark foliage. Australian silver rush *(Juncus polyanthemos)* is a tall plant with delicately thin leaves that stretch to 4 feet tall. The spires of red cardinal flower make a brilliant accent against the soft blue-gray foliage of this rush. California gray rush *(Juncus patens)* is similar but stands at attention. The horizontally striped leaves of banded bulrush (*Schoenplectus tabernaemontana* 'Zebrinus') create a sun-dappled effect in a water or bog garden.

If you want to try some moisture-loving plants, but nature hasn't provided you with a wet spot, you can make your own by burying a child's preformed plastic swimming pool and filling it with soil. The plastic lining makes it easy to control the moisture in the soil to create a bog garden. A plastic bucket works on a smaller scale. On the patio, you can grow plants such as papyrus (*Cyperus* spp.), whose roots need to be in water, by planting in a clay pot, then placing the pot inside a plastic bucket and keeping the bucket filled with water.

Grasses for Xeriscaping and Dry Sites

Drought-tolerant grasses are increasingly in demand as homeowners become more aware of the need to conserve water. They include cool-season grasses that evolved where a dose of winter or spring rainfall is followed by months of dryness and warm-season grasses from the prairies, whose extensive root systems make the most of limited rainfall. Many of these drought-tolerant plants are clump-forming rather than running grasses, each clump claiming a territory from which its spreading roots draw reserves of water. If you live in a dry climate, remember to keep fire safety in mind when planting grasses near the house, particularly cool-season grasses, which dry out in the summer.

Drought-tolerant grasses do more than just survive dry conditions. The cool-season *Stipa* grasses are beautiful, shimmering plants. Purple three-awn *(Aristida purpurea),* a native of the dry Southwest, is a beautiful grass to combine with native wildflowers such as desert marigold and globe mallow. It has filmy, gray-green foliage and panicles with long, silken hairs that catch the light. Another gardenworthy western native is Indian rice grass *(Oryzopsis hymenoides),* whose wiry sprays of seed heads bring birds to the garden. By June it acquires a golden straw color that lights up a naturalistic planting. Drought-tolerant junipers make the perfect backdrop.

Grasses that evolved on the prairies often have huge root systems and do well in gardens where rainfall is scant because of huge root systems. Plants like Indian grass *(Sorghastrum nutans)* and big bluestem *(Andropogon gerardii)* are good tall-grass species for dry gardens. Shortgrass prairie types, such as buffalo grass and blue grama *(Bouteloua gracilis),* though sometimes only 4 inches tall, have root systems that may reach

Grasses for dry sites

Andropogon gerardii (Big bluestem)
Aristida purpurea (Purple three-awn)
Bouteloua spp. (Grama grasses)
Buchloe dactyloides (Buffalo reed grass)
Dasylirion texanum (Sotol)
Deschampsia spp. (Hair grass)
Eragrostis spp. (Love grass)
Festuca gautieri (Bearskin fescue)
Festuca glauca (Blue fescue)
Koeleria macrantha (Crested hair grass)
Muhlenbergia spp. (Muhly grass)
Oryzopsis hymenoides (Indian rice grass)
Pennisetum spp. (Fountain grass)
Poa compressa (Australian blue grass)
Sorghastrum nutans (Indian grass)
Stipa spp. (Feather grasses)
Yucca filamentosa (Adam's needle)

4 feet long. All the grama grasses flourish in dry gardens. Side-oats grama *(Bouteloua curtipendula)* naturalizes easily with native wildflowers and is appealing with gray-leaved artemisias. Its seeds dangle like a row of little bells from only one side of the stem.

Growing Ornamental Grasses

If all plants were as easy to grow as grasses, we'd have little excuse to putter around the garden. They adapt to a wide range of climates and soils, need little or no maintenance, and resist almost all pests and diseases. A grass chosen with the conditions of your garden in mind will reward you with many years of unfailing good health and good looks and require almost nothing in return.

Choose Wisely

Although adaptability is one of grass's strongest points, selecting a grass with your climate, soil, and sun or shade conditions in mind is important if you want your plant to grow its best. As you read the following general suggestions on selection, keep in mind that the encyclopedia provides specific requirements of the grasses in this book.

Many of the most popular grasses will tolerate minimum temperatures found in much of the continental United States. These grasses are likely to die back in cold-winter climates and stay evergreen where winters are mild. Striped giant reed, for example, is evergreen in Zones 8 to 10 but freezes to beige in climates below Zone 8 before it regrows in spring. Hardiness zones indicate only the lowest temperatures a plant can survive. For some grasses, the quality of summer heat is a more important factor than minimum temperatures. Many will thrive in hot, dry summers but languish in humidity. Others need moist summer air to flourish.

Most, but not all, grasses prefer full sun. Sun lovers like prairie dropseed *(Sporobolus heterolepsis)* flop sadly in shade. Crinkled hair grass *(Deschampsia flexuosa),* on the other hand, thrives in cool, dim light. Ornamental grasses are adaptable to a wide range of soils, some thriving equally well in sand, clay, or perfect loam. Many perform best in average garden soil but will tolerate adverse conditions. Sedges and rushes, for example, will tolerate average garden conditions, but generally grow taller and more robust in wet soils. As mentioned in the previous chapter, the rich soil of a garden bed can be more problematic than poor soil, inducing too much growth and producing floppy plants.

A good way to ensure that your plants are a match for your climate and conditions is to grow species native to your region. They can be just as beautiful as those developed by breeders or brought from overseas. Visit sites in the wild similar to those you have or wish to create on your property and see what grows there. With the landowner's permission, you might bring home a plant. Otherwise, order from one of the steadily increasing number of suppliers specializing in native plants.

Maintenance isn't much of a factor in selecting grasses. Most require little maintenance to look good and less to stay healthy. In fact, most grasses need attention only once a year, when old foliage is removed from dormant plants to make way for new growth. (You might even dispense with that; in the wild, of course, new growth comes right up through the old.) If you are growing cool-season grasses in a border, you may want to remove dormant foliage earlier if it detracts from nearby plants making a show during the summer and fall. Some grasses, such as variegated Japanese silver grass *(Miscanthus sinensis* 'Variegatus'), spill over under their own weight. This can be a beautiful effect along a fence, but where a stiffer backbone is required, be prepared to cut off the flopped foliage and let the plant regrow from the roots, which it will do in a few weeks.

Selecting for fire safety

Dry grasses make excellent tinder, a danger for gardeners in the West, where fires are a natural part of the ecological cycle. Fire-safety guidelines for landscaping call for plants that provide a minimum amount of potential fuel. A giant clump of miscanthus feeds a fire much better than a low tuft of fescue. Cool-season grasses are often dry and dormant during brushfire season. If fire is a problem in your area, avoid summer-dormant grasses such as *Stipa* varieties, and cut back the foliage of any grasses you grow to 4 inches as soon as it ripens.

Safety guidelines for fire-prone areas recommend that 30 feet separate your house from vegetation, and many landscapers discourage planting grasses within 70 feet of the house. Outside this buffer zone, plantings of perennials, shrubs, and grasses should be staggered into self-contained, well-separated island beds. A low hedge of ornamental grass weaving through your garden is a red-carpet route that flames will follow to your door.

Invasive plants and noxious weed

Planting a rampant growing grass can initiate a life-long struggle, and these plants are usually best avoided. But some invasive grasses have their uses. Their wantonness can be an asset in naturalized plantings like meadows and prairies, or where a quick ground cover is needed. Even so, it is foolhardy to plant invasive grasses that offer no methods of control. Some can be reined in by in-ground barriers that impede the spread of rhizomes or stolons. Those that spread by seed may be restricted by cold winters, which kill the seed, or by mulching or hand weeding. Adverse soil conditions or the proximity of strong, competitive plants can retard some otherwise rampant grasses, such as blue Lyme grass (*Elymus arenarius* 'Glaucus').

A few invasive grasses have escaped the confines of gardens and fields to become bona fide pests. Readers in the South and West will be familiar with Johnson grass, introduced in the 1830s for its promise as a superior hay crop and now a noxious headache. While we haven't included noxious weeds in this book, some grasses that behave respectably in certain conditions become problems in others. The African grasses known as feathertop *(Pennisetum villosum)* and natal grass *(Rhychelytrum repens)* are well behaved in cold climates where their seeds aren't viable. In warm climates, however, they self-seed prolifically and should be avoided. If you have any doubt about a grass you're planting, consult a local nursery or extension agent.

Acquiring Grasses

As noted in the first chapter, most garden centers stock at least a few of the most popular grasses, such as miscanthus, blue fescues, pampas grass, and fountain grass. Versatile, beautiful, and easy to grow, these selections are perfect for beginners. Fortunate readers may live near a nursery specializing in grasses, where you can see a wider range of grasses before making your choices. For the widest selection of grasses, consult the list of specialty mail-order nurseries in the back of this book.

Gardeners like to pass along samples of their favorite plants to friends and family. This can be a boon to your garden and pocketbook, but be wary. Like perennials, the grasses you get over the gate are probably the most rampant growers in the garden, with wandering roots. That's how they multiply fast enough to provide divisions to pass along. The root masses of more self-contained clumping species usually knit together into an impenetrable whole that requires the vigorous use of an axe to hack off divisions. Even a favorite neighbor probably won't go to that length to hand you a sample (though you may be handed the axe).

The grasses you buy at garden centers and from some mail-order suppliers will be potted in containers. Buying plants in containers is a great idea for busy gardeners. The plants can sit in their pots for weeks or even months without damage, until you have a chance to set them into the garden. All you have to do is water them. You'll have a choice between very young plants in containers as small as 4 inches across or mature landscape-ready specimens in huge plastic tubs. Before you succumb to the instant gratification of big plants, consider that grasses grow rapidly to full size. If you can wait a year or two, your young plant will catch up to the much more expensive older specimen.

Most mail-order nurseries ship their plants bare-root. Sent while dormant, these plants arrive unpotted, with a small ball of soil or some moisture-retaining material around the roots. First-time mail-order buyers are often dismayed when their first purchases arrive. A spindly plant of switch grass may show only a few stems of leaves, yet its roots may dangle a foot long and in such a thick bunch you can't get your hand around them. Remember that the plant is dormant and that grasses put their effort into growing far-reaching roots before their tops begin to flourish.

Bare-root plants should be planted as soon as possible. Specify an arrival date that suits your schedule, or have the plants delivered to your place of business so they don't sit on a sunny doorstep for hours waiting for you to get home from

Grasses to grow from seed

These grasses are especially easy to grow from seed.

Bouteloua curtipendula
Bouteloua gracilis
Briza media
Coix lacryma-jobi
Eragrostis curvula
Eragrostis spectabilis
Eragrostis trichoides 'Bend'
Erianthus ravennae
Hordeum jubatum
Hystrix patula
Koeleria spp.
Lagurus ovatus

Melica spp.
Oryzopsis milliacea
Panicum spp.
Pennisetum setaceum
Pennisetum villosum
Rhychelytrum repens
Sorghastrum nutans
Stipa spp.
Tridens falvus
Tripsicum dactyloides
Zea mays

work. Unpack the plants right away and inspect the roots. If they're dried out, broken, rotted, or diseased, call the supplier (reputable firms will replace damaged plants). If the plant looks healthy and you just need a few hours to prepare a planting hole, wrap the roots in very moist paper towels or pop them in a bucket of water. If you haven't decided on a permanent home for the plants, set each one into a good-sized pot of soil and water it in well. Then you can transplant when you're ready, in a week or a month.

Growing ornamental grasses from seed is inexpensive and fun, and every year it seems catalogs offer more choices. (Annual grasses are sometimes listed under "everlastings" in catalogs.) Remember, however, that a plant grown from seed may not reproduce the exact traits of its parents, which is why most ornamental grasses are propagated by division. Blue Lyme grass *(Elymus arenarius),* for example, is fairly easy to start from seed, but the seedlings may range from green to gray to steel blue in color. Some plants set infertile seed; others are slow to germinate or slow to reach mature size from seed. The list above includes good selections to grow from seed.

When to plant

Warm-season grasses do best if planted in early spring so they become established before the punishing heat of summer. If you transplant in summer, be generous with the watering hose and rig up some temporary shade for new plants for the first couple of weeks. Except in mild-winter areas, fall planting is unwise because it generally doesn't allow time for roots to establish themselves enough to resist being heaved out of the ground during freeze-thaw cycles. A thick blanket of mulch or a constant cover of deep snow may help insulate the soil and the crown of the plant enough to carry it through the winter, but why chance it. Cool-season grasses can be placed in the ground in spring, summer, or fall. If you plant in fall, be aware that the aboveground portion of the grass may not come to life until late winter or early spring; but the unseen roots will be busy settling in.

Preparing a Site for Planting

Not the least of the attractions of ornamental grasses is the ease with which they can be planted. You seldom have to improve the drainage, fertility, or tilth of your soil before planting, particularly if you've chosen grasses adapted to your climate and soil conditions. New beds and borders or larger plantings such as meadows and prairies will take some muscle power, but mainly to remove turf or weeds. (You can even plant clumping types directly into existing vegetation without clearing or tilling the soil.) You can choose among the following methods for clearing a new planting bed based on the size of the bed, the type of vegetation to remove, and the amount of time you can invest.

Stripping off existing turf

For mixed beds or borders where lawn now grows, you can remove the turf by either hand or machine. With a sharp spade, you can remove sod from a 5-foot by 20-foot bed in an afternoon. Rent a power sod cutter (available from most home and garden rental businesses) for larger areas. The machine, which peels long strips of sod about 18 inches wide, is about as easy to handle as a rotary tiller.

To strip sod by hand, first remove tap-rooted weeds such as dandelions, dock, or Queen-Anne's-lace. (Do this before power stripping, too.) Outline a strip of turf about 18 inches wide and 3 feet to 4 feet long by making vertical cuts 3 inches to 4 inches deep with a flat spade. Working in from the edges of the strip, slice horizontally through the roots. Roll the loosened strip backward upon itself, exactly as you would roll up a rug. Keep your dandelion digger handy to free clinging roots. Repeat the procedure as needed. You can transplant the turflike sod or cut it into smaller pieces, shake out loose soil onto the planting bed, then compost the remainder. Turn the pieces upside down so that the grass dies and rots.

Smothering vegetation

A slower but less laborious method than stripping sod, smothering vegetation blocks air and sunlight to kill grass and weeds. Use sheets of black plastic, thick overlapping sections of newspaper, or an 8- to 10-inch layer of dense mulch such as clean straw, grass clippings, or chopped leaves. Smothering a bed can take much longer than stripping sod, up to several months. During a hot summer, however, a plastic mulch can kill vegetation in less than a week.

A combination of stripping and smothering will work well if you're planting a bed of widely spaced ornamental grasses. Strip the sod from the immediate planting areas around the grasses, then smother the rest of the bed with newspaper topped by a deep layer of organic mulch.

Cultivation

Tilling under unwanted vegetation with a rotary or tractor tiller will kill many existing plants. Repeat the tilling at least three times, about a week apart, to kill survivors and seedlings that will germinate from dormant seeds brought to life by disturbing the site. Tilling is not a good method for sites infested with quack grass, Bermuda grass, Johnson grass, or other rhizomatous plants whose severed rhizomes will quickly produce new plants.

Chemical eradication

For large-scale plantings, such as meadow or prairie gardens, the most practical solution may be to apply a glyphosate-based herbicide, sold as Roundup, Kleenup, or Ranger. Highly toxic, these compounds kill all types of vegetation on the site, but break down completely in a relatively short period after application. (Organic gardeners can use the methods above to clear and plant small parts of the larger area, until eventually the whole site is planted.) Apply exactly as the label directs on a windless day, and expect the vegetation to begin turning brown in about 10 days. Wait several weeks to see if weeds reappear and warrant another application. Herbicides are effective against quack and Bermuda grass infestations, but the tenacious Johnson grass has been known to resist even agricultural-strength chemical assassins.

Soil amendments

Some of the grasses you want to grow may require improvements in your soil's fertility or drainage. With grasses, it's best not to be too generous, which encourages rapid, weaker growth. But digging in an inch or two of compost or aged manure at planting time will reward you with lush, healthy young plants that quickly make a splash in the garden. These immature grasses will fill in more quickly if their roots can pull in liberal amounts of nutrients.

In areas of clay soil, where water is likely to collect in wintertime, you can improve drainage by working in liberal amounts of sand and compost before planting. (Be aware that adding too little sand to heavy clay can produce concretelike soil.) These amendments will also raise the area of your planting bed above the surrounding soil, creating a mounded bed effect that helps water drain away from the rot-vulnerable crowns of the plants.

Planting

Dig a hole, plop in a plant, fill in the hole, water, and presto! Although planting is a simple process, we offer the following pointers to help ensure a successful and appealing result.

Spacing

Adequate elbow room is important for the looks and health of any plant. Clumping grasses have such distinctive forms that most are best appreciated when they have room to breathe. Crowded plants are also more susceptible to fungal disease. A general rule of thumb is to base the spacing on the mature height of the plant — if a miscanthus reaches 4 feet tall, plant the next specimen 4 feet away, measuring from the center of one plant to the center of the next. Spacing is not a science. Some gardeners allow a little extra room, while others prefer the look of plants that overlap and flow upon one another. In addition to considering space between plants, you should consider space between plants and people. Hanging into walkways or paths, grass blades can be annoying ticklers or downright dangerous if they possess sharp-edged leaves.

Planting container-grown and bare-root grasses

It's easy to plant container-grown plants. Dig a hole big enough to accommodate the root ball, fill it with water, and let the water soak into the surrounding soil. Turn the pot upside down with your hand across the top, slip the plant out, and put the root ball into the hole. Fill the hole with soil, firm it into place, and water the plant thoroughly with a gentle spray or slow trickle. This technique works for planting into a prepared bed or for planting a specimen in the lawn or other existing vegetation.

If roots encircle the ball of soil, gently untangle them and spread them out in the planting hole. Make sure the crown of the plant sits in the hole at the same depth as in the pot or a little higher than the surrounding soil. If you bury the crown too deeply the shoots may not have enough strength

Planting Timetable	
Sow seeds in pots	Spring or summer
Sow seeds in garden	Early spring
Sow cool-season grasses	Fall, in mild-winter climates
Plant bare-root warm-season grasses	Early spring, or year-round in mild climates
Plant container-grown grasses	Early spring or summer, or year-round in mild climates
Plant container-grown or bare-root cool-season grasses	Spring or early fall

to fight their way to the surface and the depression in the soil will trap water around the crown and cause rot. If you miscalculated on the depth of the hole, lift the plant out (slide your hand under the root ball, don't grab the foliage or crown), and add and firm soil in the hole until you reach the necessary height. Firm it down before final planting so it doesn't settle excessively later.

After watering in the new transplant, you can spread a thin layer of compost or aged manure over the soil surface around the plant, to a distance of 8 to 10 inches from the crown, but the extra nutrients aren't really necessary. To help retain moisture, mulch very young plants with an inch or two of grass clippings or other organic matter, and older transplants (from gallon pots) with 2 to 3 inches of organic material. Keep the crown of the plant free of mulch.

Plant bare-root grasses in much the same way as container plants, as soon as possible after they arrive. Trim off dead or damaged roots, then support the plant in the hole with one hand as you work soil around the roots with the other. Make sure the crown is at the level of the surrounding soil or slightly above.

Direct seeding

Some annual grasses are quick to sprout and can be sown directly in a bed or border like a pack of marigolds. Following the timetable and depth directions on the seed packet, simply sprinkle the seeds onto bare, loosened soil and keep them moist until germination. Watch for competing weeds that may arise, and snip them off with manicure scissors at the base, to avoid disturbing the grass roots. Hare's tail *(Lagurus ovatus)* is an excellent grass to sow directly into the border. The endearing fuzzy heads are charming in a mixed planting of flowers and grasses. Tender fountain grass *(Pennisetum setaceum),* which is treated as an annual in cold-winter climates, is another rewarding grass to seed in place. (We'll discuss how to seed a large area, such as a meadow or prairie, later in the chapter.)

Planting seeds in pots

Perennial grasses are best sown in pots, then transplanted into the garden. Not only do many perennials take longer than annuals to germinate, the little plants are easy to lose track of in the garden. The techniques are much the same as the ones you use to start vegetables or perennials from seed. Consult the packet for any special requirements (some seeds need to be refrigerated, for example). Sow two to four seeds in a 3- or 4-inch plastic pot or a deep, skinny pot or cell-pack that allows the roots to extend downward naturally instead of coiling around the walls. Keep the seeds moist until germination, then place the little seedlings under lights or in a bright window. Unlike vegetables or perennials which need to be thinned to only one plant in the pot, all of these little grass plants may be left to form a clump.

When the seedlings are several inches tall, harden them off before planting in the garden, just as you would annual or perennial flower seedlings. This process involves exposing the plant to outdoor conditions away from the wind a little at a time over several weeks, at first for an hour, then for a couple of hours, then half a day, then all day, then finally for several days. You'll usually notice a visible change in color and texture as the grass leaves toughen up to meet outdoor conditions. Fertilizer should be cut back about two weeks before you move the plants outside, then stopped altogether in the last week or several days.

Planting on a slope

Instead of stripping away existing vegetation and exposing soil to erosion from rain and wind, you can smother unwanted plants on a slope with a thick layer of newspaper or mulch and plant container-grown grasses through the mulch. The old vegetation holds the soil but doesn't compete for water or nutrients while the new grasses become established. If you must strip away old vegetation, spread a heavy organic mulch (about 4 inches thick) and plant through it as soon as possible. You'll need about 1 cubic yard of mulch to cover 100 square feet to that depth.

Start planting at the top of the slope, setting plants more closely together than you would in a border to prevent damage from erosion. Build up soil on the down-slope side of each planting hole so you can place the plant's crown level, instead of following the slope's incline. On steep slopes, push a wooden shingle into the soil or nestle a stone on the down-slope side to prevent the soil from washing away before the roots take hold. As a further erosion-control measure, drip irrigate the plants. If you don't have a drip hose, set a plastic milk jug next to each plant, and poke a small hole in the bottom to release water slowly into the soil.

The techniques described later in the chapter for direct-seeding a meadow or prairie will also work for a slope, just take extra care with mulching and watering to avoid erosion.

Planting in boggy soil or water

Installing plants in ponds or wet, boggy soil will take you back to the days when you played in puddles or made mud pies. The task is as simple and as messy. For a large boggy area, old clothes are advisable, along with a pair of high rubber boots and two squares of plywood large enough to support your weight. A 2-foot square should support up to 150 pounds, a 3-foot square anyone heavier. You can use them like stepping stones as you move through the wet soil, using a long-handled hoe to move one square out of the muck while you stand on the other.

To plant, scoop out a hole big enough for the roots or root ball and refill it with the muck you removed. Placing the crown is not critical, because the water level of bogs and wetlands fluctuates, but don't bury the plant. You needn't bother with mulch or additional watering, unless you're in the middle of a prolonged dry spell.

For true water plants, such as papyrus (*Cyperus* spp.), work under water and plant into the pond bottom, if you have a soil-bottomed pond and the plants are hardy in your area. If you have a lined pond or the plants aren't hardy, plant in pots. Keeping the plants in pots makes them easy to remove both for storage in winter and when the pool needs maintenance. Suppliers selling water plants can often provide detailed instructions for planting and care. In general, common water plants will do well planted in plastic or terra cotta pots filled with heavy loam garden soil and fertilized periodically with special pellets. Cover the soil surface with coarse gravel to hold the soil in place under water. Be sure to plant or set the pots at the water depth recommended for the plant.

Establishing a prairie or meadow

The allure of a broad expanse of wildflowers and grasses, dotted with birds and butterflies, has fueled the popularity of "meadow in a can" gardens. Unfortunately, most of these efforts end in failure — establishing a sustainable meadow or prairie planting is a lot of work. Before setting out to convert a large swath of property to meadow or prairie, weigh the effort with the reward. You may decide that growing wildflowers and grasses in the more controlled confines of one or more smaller beds or borders makes more sense. We'll outline the procedures for making a meadow or prairie planting here. It is a good idea to consult with a local wildflower expert (try your nursery or extension agent) to determine the best mix of plants for your area and to find out what methods of installation, care, and maintenance have proven most successful in local conditions.

Unless you have the money to buy large quantities of container-grown plants, or the time and space to start them from seed, you'll need to direct-seed the site. (Small sites can be planted with transplants or plugs and the bare soil heavily mulched to control weeds.) Sow meadow and prairie grasses in late spring or early summer in cold climates. Most of them are warm-season plants, germinating best when soil heats up in spring. If you live in an area prone to summer drought, move the planting schedule up a few weeks. Seed in the fall in mild-winter areas where the soil stays warm year-round and rainfall is abundant following planting.

Eliminating the competitive existing vegetation is the first step to a successful meadow or prairie planting. Any of the techniques described earlier in the chapter will work, though for larger areas tilling or chemical eradication may be the most practical. These methods eliminate plants, but weed seeds will still lie in wait by the millions, ready to spring into action as soon as you till the soil. Wait a week to 10 days after tilling or cultivating the soil, and lightly hoe off any weeds that sprout. Repeat this procedure once or twice.

Once cleared, small areas can be sowed the old-fashioned way, by hand, or with a lawn-grass or fertilizer spreader. Larger areas will require a tractor; you might even want to hire a farmer with a mechanical seed drill. Seed quantities will vary depending on the mix of wildflowers and grasses you choose. In general, an acre of grasses would require 10 pounds of seed, or 1 pound per thousand square feet. Prepare the seed by mixing it with an extender, such as vermiculite, sand, sawdust, or Kitty Litter, so that it will be easy to see what areas you've already covered. Combine about 4 pounds of Kitty Litter or sand with every pound of seed. If you use dry vermiculite or sawdust, use about a 5-gallon bucketful for each half-pound of seed, and dampen the mix slightly so that the seed sticks to the extender and doesn't sift to the bottom of the bucket.

To broadcast seed by hand, scatter it with steady, even tosses. To ensure good coverage, walk and sow in parallel rows, then repeat, walking perpendicular to your first passes. After scattering the seed, rake the area lightly, so that about a quarter-inch of soil covers the seed. For a big area, wire a piece of chain-link fence fabric or stock fence behind a garden tractor and pull it across the field. Grass seeds sprout best when they're pressed firmly into the soil. A water-filled lawn roller (rented locally) is easy to handle, because you can fill it to a weight that you can manage. If you're planting a big sweep of grasses, hitch up a roller attachment to the tractor that tilled your field and go over the area thoroughly. After rolling the planted area, scatter a light covering of clean wheat or oat straw across it. Shake out any clumps so you don't impede the growth of seedling grasses. Set up overhead sprinklers and water at least an inch. To measure the amount of water, set out empty cat food or tuna cans at various places.

Water an additional quarter-inch to half-inch (depending on your weather) every other day, so that the top layer of soil stays moist and hospitable to emerging roots. You'll see green shoots within days after planting, but your new planting won't look much like a lawn. These grasses will be putting their energy into root growth, not top growth. Leave the straw in place to naturally decompose, but watch for emerging broadleaf weeds and remove the most rampant growers. Your grasses won't be able to keep pace with fast-growing annual weeds, and you'll find it impossible to weed the whole area. So, when the weeds reach about 8 inches high, mow with the blade set at about 4 inches, to knock the weeds back and let sunlight reach the seedling grasses. When the weeds regrow to that 8-inch height, check the height of your grass seedlings, then set the mower accordingly and mow again. Those fast-growing weeds are annuals, and it may take three mowings or more the first season to knock them down to size.

If your new meadow or prairie includes wildflowers as well as grasses, you'll have to depend on hand-pulling the worst of the weeds until your flowers bloom and set seed. A mowing before then would knock the wildflowers back (particularly fast-growing annuals) and probably kill off quite a few. Once the wildflowers have set seed, mowing the meadow will bring light to young grasses and help to scatter the flower seeds. Check the height of your grasses and set the mower just above them. As a bonus, some of your flowers may put forth another round of bloom.

Ongoing Care

Grasses are the ultimate low-maintenance plant. Most will do very well with no supplemental feeding or watering, and they rarely get sick. But to keep them looking their best they may need the gardener's hand several times a year.

Watering and feeding

Most perennial grasses are drought-tolerant once established, but annual grasses, lacking extensive root systems, always appreciate water, and so do perennials in their first year of life. Water annuals as you would any flowers in the annual garden, about an inch a week. If rainfall is generous, they may need no supplemental watering. Water newly transplanted perennials every other day or every three days in well-drained garden soil. If your soil is light in texture or heavy in clay content, adjust your watering accordingly.

Additional water after the first year is not essential for perennials, but it will result in a lush plant that is taller and wider than usual. In drought conditions a grass may reach only half to two-thirds the size it does in a well-watered garden. But because grasses generally adapt to prevailing conditions, it's better not to start watering established plants in the spring if you don't plan to continue watering all season long — they'll suffer when the hose is withdrawn.

To provide supplemental water to established grasses, use soaker hoses or drip irrigation, or lay a garden hose directly at the plant's base. Overhead sprinklers are inefficient in delivering water directly to the roots and lose too much to evaporation. In humid climates they may also cause disease.

Grasses don't benefit from supplemental feeding, and they can in fact be hurt by it. Too much nitrogen can lead to either weak or rampant growth.

Staking

Some of the most beautiful grasses have a weak backbone that may not withstand uncommonly strong winds or other extremes of weather. Others will flop over from their own weight or size. To keep them standing erect, drive sturdy supports, such as thin metal pipes, into the earth and bind them with a cat's-cradle of strong twine or a loop of plastic-coated wire. Allow the plants some freedom of movement within the support so that they don't look like they're standing in a straitjacket. The stakes can be camouflaged with green paint and hidden from view among the foliage.

Cutting back

Until recently, many gardeners trimmed back ornamental grasses as part of the fall cleanup. But a new appreciation of the beauty of weathering foliage, flowers, and seed heads has prolonged their presence through the winter, cut back earlier only if they become tattered or bare-looking. Most people cut back old foliage before new growth starts in spring, around the time early spring bulbs show their first shoots. Cool-season grasses can be cut back after they die out in the summer garden if you find their brown leaves unsightly. Often a stiff raking will be enough to remove old foliage. Grasses can also be cut back at other times of the year for other reasons. If, for example, a clump of miscanthus grass flops after a heavy rainstorm and doesn't recover in a few days, cut it back and it will shoot up again quickly.

While tolerance for untidiness dictates when and whether to cut grasses back, how much to cut can determine the future good health of your plant. As a general rule, don't cut grasses too short — in most cases that means leaving at least 4 inches of stubble. If you cut any shorter, you run the risk of clipping emerging new shoots that are hidden among the old stems, giving their tips a tattered look from which they won't recover. Leaving a few inches of old foliage also protects the crown and new shoots from weather extremes. Before you start slicing, pull apart the clump and check for emerging green shoots among the dead foliage. If you've missed on the timing, it won't hurt to cut a little higher than usual.

Effective grass cutters include hand shears or a trimmer with a metal blade (grass leaves tend to wrap around a string trimmer and jam it). Some gardeners take a chainsaw to particularly dense clumps. Keep a sharpening stone handy. The silica in grass rubs like sandpaper against the metal blades, dulling them like nothing else in the garden. Also look out for any metal supports you may have installed to help the clump stand up. They can be an unpleasant surprise when you're swinging a bladed trimmer.

Grass clippings from a spring shearing make a timely offering to garden birds for their nests. The long, dry leaves are favorites of sparrows and other songbirds. If you are handy, they can also be easily twisted into rustic wreaths, swags, or other long-lasting arrangements.

Division
Ornamental grasses can grow for decades without needing to be divided. But occasionally a clump will die out in the center and beg for renovation. Or you may want to collect a few starts from an existing plant to add elsewhere in the garden.

Running grasses are easy to divide. Using a spade or a trowel, dig up rooted pieces at any time during the growing season. Transfer them to new planting sites and water well.

Small clumping grasses aren't much more trouble. Divide them with a spade and a sharp knife in early spring when new growth begins. Just dig up the clump, wash enough soil from the roots to see what you're doing, then slice the plant into smaller pieces and transplant them.

Large clumping grasses require a lot more muscle and an arsenal of tools and gear because of their tremendous matted root systems. You'll need an axe or a wood saw instead of a shovel, gloves to protect your hands from sharp leaf blades, goggles to protect your eyes from leaf tips, and a strong back. First cut back the foliage by about a third. Dig around all sides of the plant with the shovel, slicing as deeply as you can under the roots. When the plant is loose, lever it onto its side; then either drag it to a work area or work in place. Spray off some soil from the root ball so the roots are easily visible, then hack the plant into sections with your axe or saw. Divide into still smaller pieces using a trowel or your hands. Replant the divisions quickly so the roots don't dry out.

If a plant has died out in the middle, you can try a "heart transplant" instead of digging the whole thing up and dividing it. Slice around the dead middle with a sharp spade, then pry it out with a crowbar. Add fresh soil in the center, and install a new plant of the same species.

Prairie burn

Nature maintains meadows and prairies with periodic fires, which clear accumulated debris, return nutrients in the debris to the soil, and eliminate woody and weedy invaders. Large-scale planted meadows or prairies can benefit from the same treatment every two to four years. Before contemplating a burn, do some planning. First find out if such fires are legal in your area and, if so, what precautions the fire department requires. A local wildflower or prairie restoration group or your county extension agent may be able to provide information on procedures and permits. Read a comprehensive publication on burning (try your extension service) to familiarize yourself with how it works, and then observe or help in a prairie burn before you attempt to set up your own.

Spring (late March to early May) is a good time for a burn. The warmed soil stimulates microbial activity, making nutrients available to plants, which respond with a burst of vigor. The moisture in the soil and in plants at that time of year means that a fire will move more slowly and therefore be easier to control than at other times of the year.

Start small, on half an acre or less, until you gain experience. Be sure to follow local regulations and notify neighbors and the fire department of your plans. You'll need at least three helpers to keep the fire under control. Specialized equipment to put out fires and metal rakes to spread the flames are also a must. Don't try to get by with a garden hose; you'll need a water backpack/fire pump for control of the blaze. A grass fire may look tame compared to a forest fire, but it can quickly leap out of control.

Pests and Disease

Grasses are as disease- and pest-resistant as plants can be. Rust, an unsightly fungus, is their only disease, and it's not fatal. Aphids and grasshoppers may dine on the tender new growth. But grasses are quick to recover from these attacks. A bit more bothersome are pocket gophers. They can slice through grass roots with their sharp incisors and pull an entire plant down into their network of tunnels. Gardeners in coastal California and other areas of the West have learned to foil these grass thieves by lining the sides and bottom of planting holes with baskets made of chicken wire or hardware cloth. Rabbits, deer, and groundhogs may also occasionally dine on succulent grasses, but the rate of growth of new leaves soon outpaces any damaged foliage, which you can simply snip out.

Overcrowding on the one hand, and pampered conditions on the other, may increase the chances of rust in grasses. Though seldom a major problem, the fungal disease is unsightly, showing up as orange, powdery-looking patches on leaves and stems and causing them to turn yellow or brown and die. Rust can appear suddenly in the warm wet days and cool nights of spring, but vanish as rapidly when hot, dry weather comes. Poor air circulation or overhead watering can aggravate the problem. To prevent its possible occurrence, apply wettable sulphur in spring or during a humid summer. If signs of rust are already present, immediately clip off affected leaves and dispose of them in the trash. Also remove and replace mulch around infected plants. The disease overwinters in fallen leaves and other material.

Grasses in the Landscape

Grasses fit in everywhere in the home landscape. Here, 'Karl Foerster' feather reed grass stands out against a backdrop of trees and shrubs.

*Growing 3–4 ft. tall, 'Yaku Jima' dwarf miscanthus is a
perfect specimen grass for a small garden.*

*Buffalo grass grows 4–6 in. high and makes a fine
naturalized lawn, though it goes dormant early.*

The fine-textured clumps of silver spear grass are equally at home in borders, naturalistic plantings, and near water.

A striking effect can be had with little effort or cost. A single tuft of blue oat grass adds enough contrasting color and form to set off the stand of 'Autumn Joy' sedum and the clump of feather reed grass behind.

The cool blue tones of some grasses brighten the yellows, pinks, or purples of perennials, giving these colors more mileage in the garden.

The feathery flowers of many grasses are more striking than their foliage. Long white plumes of feathertop stand out even more against the black-flowered 'Moudry' fountain grass.

This border devoted exclusively to grasses reveals their many shapes, sizes, and colors.

*The last hurrah of summer, tall and mid-height grasses form
a lush backdrop for the pincushion pods and woody stems of
spent perennials. The grasses will continue to bleach silver
and tan as fall and winter approach.*

Botanical gardens and public landscaping sometimes offer imaginative grass plantings, like this border of grasses at Kew Gardens, in London, for ideas and specimens to incorporate into your own garden.

This "wild" border planted with grasses re-creates the sweep of nature's bounty.

'Gracillimus' maiden grass provides a background of fine green foliage for the airy panicles of variegated moor grass. Pairing grasses of substantial mass can have as great an impact as pairing grasses with shrubs.

Grass plumes left to weather in the winter landscape serve as a picturesque platform for snow.

Silver-leaved miscanthus contrasts with the low-growing greenery in the foreground and bridges the transition to tall shrubs and trees in the background.

Treat grasses just like perennials in the mixed border, taking into account bloom time and height in relation to other plants.

The bright ribbons of Eulalia grass contrast in the late summer border with rusty red sedum.

Tall miscanthus grasses frame the modern lines of this raised patio and balcony and serve as attractive screens as well as points of interest.

The fine blades of 'Gracillimus' maiden grass are a perfect counterpoint to the flowers of the neighboring perennials.

Arching grasses grown in a pot can create the effect of a fountain. Even substantial grasses, like this crimson fountain grass, will readily adapt to life in a container.

Reflections in still water double the display of this evergreen miscanthus. Its reddish plumes will turn golden brown in fall.

Variegated miscanthus brightens the mostly green perennial border in late spring.

The metallic color of blue Lyme grass combines well with almost all perennials, but, like other running grasses, it has a tendency to overrun the perennial border.

The panicles of tufted hair grass reach up to 5 ft. high, but their delicacy and the low mounding habit of the foliage make this grass a good choice near the front of the border. Cool-season grasses like this one bloom in early summer, when other perennials are hitting their stride.

A bed of grasses in a farm garden takes on tones of silver and gold under a coating of frost. Many ornamental grasses keep color and form alive in the winter landscape.

The shimmer of fountain grass above coleus and geraniums shows off these common annuals in a new way. You can grow tender perennial and annual grasses just as you would flowering annuals.

Ribbon grass is right at home in the annual border with snapdragons, salvia, heliopsis, and cosmos. Running grasses are usually not well enough behaved to be invited into the perennial border.

Lattice and brick create a handsome backdrop for the flowing fountain grass and the fiery 'Crimson Pygmy' barberry.

The ghostly shape of variegated miscanthus becomes the centerpiece of this wooded garden of hostas and foxgloves.

Many of the blue grasses, like this blue oat grass, are excellent plants to combine with spring bulbs — their fresh new growth complements the bulb flowers, and they soon grow to cover the yellowing bulb leaves.

Beds of ivy, tufted hair grass, and other grasslike ground covers light up a shady entry from late spring through summer.

*Scattered among perennials and succulents on a rocky
hillside, the sword-shaped clumps of grasslike New Zealand
flax bring a wild look to the landscape.*

The first in the wild to inhabit the most inhospitable sites, highly adaptable grasses are indispensable in a naturalistic setting.

Grasses are a natural around water. Fine-leaved sprays of contrasting colors add a fountainlike effect to this quiet lily pond.

Rock pools below this shaded gazebo are a natural setting
for spearlike cattails and spidery umbrella plants grown in
the water.

Mature stands of dwarf fountain grass lend a formal symmetry to the corners of this rectangular pool. The freely flowering grass plumes can be cut for fresh arrangements.

The earth tones of these clumps of fountain grass reflect the colors of the desert.

Mounding and tufted grasses are self-contained enough for rock gardens. Many of the drought-tolerant varieties used in dry gardens are cool-season western natives that go dormant in summer.

Gallery of Grasses

The photographs in this section will help you to put a "face" to the plants discussed in the essays and encyclopedia. They are organized alphabetically by genus and species. A short description accompanies each photo, along with the plant's botanical and common names, height, hardiness zone rating, and the page on which you'll find its encyclopedia entry.

A Word About Color

Color, more than many other visual attributes, is in the eye of the beholder. What one person describes as blue, another may call lavender, or even purple. Compounding these differences of opinion are the effects of light and shade, time of day, and nearby colors on what we actually see. Grasses exhibit a narrower range of colors than more flamboyantly flowering plants, but this in some ways complicates the problem, requiring us to distinguish among a myriad of greens, blue-greens, buffs, browns, and golds.

As you look at the photos on the following pages, remember that the camera, no less than the eye, captures color as it appears at a certain moment and season. Add to that the natural variation among plants and the difficulty of printing colors precisely, and you'll see why it doesn't pay to count on your plant having exactly the color you see in the photograph.

| *Achnatherum* *calamagrostis* | *Silver spear grass* *Height 18–36 in.* *Clumping grass* *with fluffy flower* *heads that persist* *through winter* *Zone 6–9* | *Good for borders,* *naturalistic* *plantings, along* *water or ponds* *p. 182* |

| *Acorus calamus* 'Variegatus' | *Variegated sweet* *flag* *Height: 2–3 ft.* *Bold foliage, stripes* *can be creamy* *white to yellow* *Zones 5–10* | *Use for accent in* *moist to wet soils* *or in water* *p. 184* |

Acorus gramineus 'Ogon'

Golden variegated Japanese sweet flag Height: 10 in. Use as accent or mass planting in garden or by pond Zones 6–9

Sun or part sun; good container plant. p. 184

Agropyron magellanicum

Blue Magellan grass Height: 12–18 in. Similar to blue Lyme grass without invasiveness Zones 5–8

Not suited for hot, humid conditions p. 186

| *Ammophila breviligulata* | *American beach grass*
Height: 2–3 ft.
Evergreen ground cover for sandy soils
Zones 4–7 | *Use for naturalistic plantings on coastal sites*
p. 187 |

| *Andropogon gerardii* | *Big bluestem*
Height: 4–8 ft.
Foliage and flowering stalks striking in summer and fall
Zones 4–9 | *Use as accent in large border or massed*
p. 188 |

Andropogon saccharoides

*Silver bluestem
Height: 12–18 in.
Southwest native;
seed heads
attractive when
backlit
Zones 5–9*

*Lovely in a
meadow planting
p. 189*

Aristida purpurea

*Purple three-awn
Height: 12–30 in.
Flowering stems
turn from purple to
bleached blond
Zones 6–9*

*Good for
naturalized
plantings in dry
conditions
p. 190*

Arrhenatherum elatius var. **bulbosum** 'Variegatum'	*Variegated bulbous oat grass*	*Good for front to middle of mixed border*
	Height: 8–24 in.	
	Narrow leaves have thin green stripe; flowers not decorative	*p. 191*
	Zones 4–9	

Arundinaria viridistriata	*Running bamboo*	*Use as ground cover where spread can be contained*
	Height: 30 in.	
	New leaves gold with green stripes	*p. 192*
	Zone 4	

Arundo donax

Giant reed
Height: 9–25 ft.
Fall bloom in mild
climates
Zones 6–10

Good accent plant
with water features
p. 193

Arundo donax
'Variegata'

Striped giant reed
Height: 5–12 ft.
Leaf color turns
greener during
season
Zones 8–10

Evergreen in mild
climates
p. 194

Bambusa oldhamii

*Giant timber
bamboo
Height: 50–55 ft.
Clumping bamboo
with stems up to 4
in. thick
Zone 8*

*Use like trees to
mark entry or for
screening
p. 194*

Bouteloua curtipendula

*Sideoats grama
Height: 2–3 ft.
Clump-forming;
flowering stalks in
early summer
Zones 4–9*

*Meadow or prairie
plantings
p. 195*

Bouteloua gracilis

*Blue grama grass
Height 8–24 in.
Seed heads
decorative for long
period
Zones 3–10*

*Best in mass
plantings
p. 196*

Briza media

*Perennial quaking
grass
Height: 2–3 ft.
Green spring
flowers turn tan
with age
Zones 4–8*

*Good front- or
mid-border plant
p. 197*

Buchloe
dactyloides

Buffalo grass
Height: 4–6 in.
Flowers
insignificant; greens
up late, browns
early
Zones 3–9

Good for
naturalized lawn
p. 198

Calamagrostis
acutiflora
'Karl Foerster'

'Karl Foerster'
feather reed grass
Height: 5–6 ft.
Tall flower stalks
showy summer
through fall
Zones 5–9

Full or part sun in
wet or dry soil
p. 199

**Calamagrostis
acutiflora** 'Stricta'

*Feather reed grass
Height: 5–7 ft.
Blooms May to
June; can be
evergreen in warm
climates
Zones 5–9*

*Use in border, as
specimen, or with
mixed grasses
p. 199*

**Calamagrostis
nutkaensis**

*Pacific reed grass
Height: 2–4 ft.
Early to midspring
flowers
Zones 8–9*

*Summer-drought-
tolerant ground
cover
p. 200*

| *Carex buchananii* | Leatherleaf sedge Height: 2 ft. Shiny reddish brown tufts in summer; rarely flowers Zone 6 | Use in border with blues and whites p. 201 |

| *Carex comans* | New Zealand hair sedge Height: 12–24 in. Fine-textured rolled leaves are green, brown, or whitish green Zones 7–9 | Good along water p. 201 |

| *Carex nigra* | *Black-flowering sedge*
Height: 6–9 in.
Unusual black flower spikes rise just above foliage in spring
Zones 4–8 | *Use as a ground cover or pond edging*
p. 203 |

| *Carex petriei* | *Dwarf brown sedge*
Height: 4–6 in.
Ever-brown ground cover; flowers add a curly effect among leaf tendrils
Zones 7–9 | *Needs moist but well-drained soil*
p. 203 |

Carex plantaginea

Plantain-leaved sedge
Height: 12–24 in.
Versatile ground cover; foliage stays green well into winter
Zones 4–9

Use as accent among woodland plants
p. 204

Carex siderosticha 'Variegata'

Creeping variegated broad-leaved sedge
Height: 12–24 in.
Grows in a sweeping colony of bold foliage
Zones 5 or 6–9

Use as a spot accent or ground cover
p. 204

Chasmanthium latifolium

*Northern sea oats
Height: 3–5 ft.
Clump-forming
perennial grass
with broad leaves
and dangling seed
heads
Zone 4*

*Use as border
accent or ground
cover on slopes or
open woodland
p. 206*

Coix lachryma-jobi

*Job's tears
Height: 3–6 ft.
Ungainly plant
grown for unusual
teardrop seeds
Zones 9–10*

*Perennial in mild
climates; plant as
annual from seed in
cold areas
p. 207*

**Cortaderia
selloana**

*Pampas grass
Height: 8 ft.
Feathery plumes
showy from late
summer through
midwinter
Zone 7*

*Nearly evergreen in
warm climates; use
as specimen,
barrier hedge, or
wind screen
p. 207*

**Cortaderia
selloana** *'Pumila'*

*Dwarf pampas
grass
Height: 4–6 ft.
Flower plumes rise
to 5 ft. in late
summer
Zones 8–10*

*Good with colorful
shrubs
p. 209*

Cortaderia selloana 'Silver Comet'

'Silver Comet' pampas grass
Height: 6–8 ft.
White-striped leaves distinguish this cultivar
Zones 7–10

Fine specimen
p. 209

Cymbopogon citratus

Lemongrass
Height: 2–6 ft.
Fragrant leaves used in tea and cooking
Zones 9–10

Tender perennial thrives in containers in cold-winter areas
p. 210

Cyperus alternifolius

*Umbrella plant
Height: 18–36 in.
Forms elegant
clumps of
umbrella-like leaves
Zones 9–10*

*A natural near
water or with bog
plants
p. 212*

Cyperus papyrus

*Egyptian papyrus
Height: 6–15 ft.
Long bracts form
arching sprays on
stout stems
Zones 9–10*

*Water garden or
patio showpiece
p. 213*

Cyperus profiler

*Dwarf papyrus
Height: 12–36 in.
Stiff bracts make
this a livelier
version of the
refined umbrella
plant
Zones 9–10*

*Good scale for
small pool or
aquarium
p. 213*

**Dasylirion
texanum**

*Sotol
Height: 2–3 ft.
Mounding plant
with slender flower
stalks up to 15 ft.
tall
Zones 8–10*

*Useful for desert
gardens; can be
grown in a
container
p. 214*

Deschampsia caespitosa

Tufted hair grass
Height: 2–3 ft.
Evergreen or
semievergreen;
blooms late spring
through summer
Zones 4–9

Excellent for mass
plantings
p. 215

Deschampsia caespitosa 'Bronzeschleier'

'Bronze Veil' tufted
hair grass
Height: 2–3 ft.
Drooping bloom
almost hides foliage
Zones 4–9

Use cut flowers in
bouquets
p. 215–216

Deschampsia caespitosa 'Goldgehange'

'Gold Pendant' tufted hair grass Height: 2–3 ft. Single plant commands attention Zones 4–9

Grow along water or in woodland garden p. 216

Elymus arenarius 'Glaucus'

Blue Lyme grass Height: 1–2 ft. Invasive mound-forming grass with sharp-tipped blue leaves Zones 4–10

Use in border with sunken barriers; controls erosion in all soils p. 218

| *Elymus condensatus* 'Canyon Prince' | 'Canyon Prince' wild rye Height: 18–24 in. Less invasive cultivar; flower spikes rise to 6 ft. Zones 7–9 | Use in mixed border or foliage garden p. 218 |

| *Elymus tritichoides* | Creeping wild rye Height: 2–4 ft. Fast-spreading native of American West Zones 7–10 | Use as ground cover or in mass plantings p. 219 |

**Equisetum
hyemale**

*Scouring rush
Height: 18–48 in.
Upright perennial
with striking bare
stems; native to wet
places but grows
anywhere
Zones 5–10*

*Dark green stems
keep their color
all year
p. 219*

Eragrostis curvula   *Weeping love grass
Height: 12–24 in.
Mounding habit;
drought-tolerant;
evergreen in mild
climates
Zones 7–10*   *Plant on slopes, in
border
p. 221*

Erianthus ravennae

*Ravenna grass
Height: 9–12 ft.
A hardy
pampaslike grass;
silky plumes last
through winter
Zones 6–10*

*Large plant for
screens or tall
border
p. 223*

Eriophorum latifolium

*Cotton grass
Height: 8–18 in.
Forms colonies of
thin spiky leaves;
woolly flowers in
spring
Zones 4–8*

*A light-hearted bog
plant for cool
gardens
p. 224*

Festuca amethystina

*Sheep's fescue
Height: 8–12 in.
Cool-season
evergreen;
gray-blue flowers
in late spring
Zones 4–8*

*Fine edging or
border plant, or as
short-lived ground
cover
p. 225*

Festuca gautieri

*Bearskin fescue
Height: 4 in.
Alpine native;
drought-tolerant
perennial
Zones 4–6*

*Plant in shady rock
gardens or in pots;
needs good
drainage
p. 226*

**Festuca glauca
'Blau Silber'**

*'Blue-Silver' fescue
Height: 8 in.
Clumping
evergreen; stands
up to summer heat
Zones 4–9*

*Edging, rock
garden, container
p. 227*

**Festuca glauca
'Elijah's Blue'**

*'Elijah's Blue'
fescue
Height: 8 in.
One of the palest
cultivars; medium
texture
Zones 4–9*

*Striking with deep
purples, reds, and
other strong-
colored flowers
p. 228*

Festuca glauca
'Sea Urchin'

'Sea Urchin' fescue
Height: 8 in.
Springy green
clump; extra-fine
texture
Zones 4–9

Interesting accent,
good edging or
ground cover
p. 228

Festuca muelleri

Mueller's fescue
Height: 6–8 in.
Cool-season
perennial; fine
green foliage
Zones 5–9

Needs light shade
in hot climates
p. 228

Glyceria maxima 'Variegata'

*Manna grass
Height: 2–6 ft.
Reedlike perennial
with erect-arching
habit; spreads fast
Zones 5–10*

*Aquatic grass for
large ponds
p. 229*

Hakonechloa macra

*Hakonechloa
Height: 12–30 in.
Japanese native
grass; green leaves
turn orange-bronze
in autumn
Zones 4–10*

*Finest shade
specimen or ground
cover; spreads
slowly
p. 230*

Hakonechloa macra 'Aureola'

Golden hakonechloa Height: 12–24 in. Cascading foliage; fall color intensifies to pink Zones 4–10

Combines with greens in shade garden p. 230

Helictotrichon sempervirens

Blue oat grass Height: 12–36 in. Large clump-forming perennial grass with spiky leaves; blue intensifies in dry soil Zones 4–9

Use as foundation plant, ground cover p. 231

Helictotrichon sempervirens 'Saphirsprundel'

'Sapphire Fountain' blue oat grass
Height: 24 in.
Dense arching tuft with clear blue-gray leaves
Zones 4–9

Superb in perennial border as single accent or massed
p. 232

Hordeum jubatum

Foxtail barley
Height: 12–30 in.
Short-lived perennial grass; distinctive flowers in early summer
Zones 4–10

Grow as annual in masses or for cut flowers
p. 232

| **Hystrix patula** | *Bottlebrush grass* *Height: 24–48 in.* *Perennial* *woodland grass;* *flowers persist* *through fall* *Zones 4–9* | *Good shade-garden* *grass* *p. 233* |

| **Imperata cylindrica 'Red Baron'** | *Japanese blood* *grass* *Height: 12–18 in.* *Perennial creeper;* *bright red foliage;* *seldom flowers* *Zones 6–9* | *Fine accent plant;* *use as edging for* *lawn or border, or* *massed on slopes* *p. 234* |

Juncus effusus

*Soft rush
Height: 18–48 in.
Expands gradually
by creeping roots
Zones 4–9*

*Adds a natural
look to water
gardens but is
adaptable to dry
soil
p. 235*

**Juncus effusus
'Spiralis'**

*Corkscrew rush
Height: 12–24 in.
Semievergreen
oddity of coiling
stems; flowers not
showy
Zones 4–9*

*Thrives in moist
locations
p. 235*

Juncus patens

*California gray rush
Height: 18–30 in.
Slender, erect form;
foliage bluish green
year-round
Zones 8–9*

*Very adaptable
p. 236*

Koeleria argentea   *Silver hair grass
Height: 12–18 in.
Cool-season
perennial;
handsome two-
toned leaves
Zones 6–9*

*Use as ground
cover in sunny,
well-drained sites
p. 236*

Koeleria glauca

*Large blue hair grass
Height: 6–24 in.
Dainty evergreen tufts; best in lean, sandy soil
Zones 6–9*

*Use for edging or massing
p. 237*

Koeleria macrantha

*Crested hair grass
Height: 12–18 in.
Perennial; erect tufted habit; variable gray-green color
Zones 2–9*

*Use in naturalistic meadow
p. 237*

Lagurus ovatus

Hare's tail
Height: 12–24 in.
Soft green tufts go
unnoticed once
blooms appear in
summer
All zones

Grow from seed in
annual bed; use in
cut-flower
arrangements
p. 238

Luzula nivea
'Snowbird'

'Snow Bird' snowy
wood rush
Height: 8–12 in.
Forms small
clumps of velvety
gray leaves
Zones 4–9

Fine perennial for
shade or woodland
garden
p. 238

Melica ciliata   *Hairy melic grass, silky spike melic*
Height: 8–12 in.
Perennial cool-season; flowers in late spring or early summer
Zones 5–8

For casual border or cut flowers
p. 240

Miscanthus floridulus   *Giant Chinese silver grass*
Height: 8–12 ft.
Pyramidal flower plumes in fall
Zones 5–9

Use as specimen, hedge, or windbreak; needs no staking
p. 242

**Miscanthus
sacchariflorus**

*Silver banner grass
Height: 4–8 ft.
Foliage turns tan;
flowers attractive
for months;
invasive
Zones 5–9*

*Good for wet
meadow or pond
edging
p. 243*

**Miscanthus
sinensis** 'Cabaret'

*'Cabaret'
miscanthus
Height: 6–8 ft.
Pink blooms in
early fall
Zones 7–10*

*Use as specimen,
border backdrop,
screen
p. 245*

**Miscanthus
sinensis
'Cosmopolitan'**

*'Cosmopolitan'
miscanthus
Height: 6–8 ft.
Abundant coppery
red plumes in fall;
needs no staking
Zones 7–10*

*Large specimen or
accent
p. 245*

**Miscanthus
sinensis
'Flamingo'**

*'Flamingo'
miscanthus
Height: 5–6 ft.
Lush foliage; long
feathery plumes
Zones 6–9*

*Use as specimen or
along water
p. 245*

Miscanthus sinensis 'Gracillimus'

Maiden grass
Height: 5–8 ft.
Copper-red tassels
in midautumn
Zones 5–9

Grow as specimen;
may need support
p. 246

Miscanthus sinensis 'Graziella'

'Graziella'
miscanthus
Height: 5–6 ft.
Fine leaf texture;
summer-blooming
Zones 5–9

Smaller miscanthus
for mixed border
p. 246

**Miscanthus
sinensis 'Kascade'**

*'Cascade'
miscanthus
Height: 5–7 ft.
Blooms early and
for long periods
Zones 5–8*

*Good in mixed
border; specimen
grouping; near
water
p. 246*

**Miscanthus
sinensis
'Kleine Fontaine'**

*'Little Fountain'
miscanthus
Height: 3–4 ft.
Compact grass;
extended bloom
time
Zones 6–9*

*Excellent in front
of taller grasses or
in the mid-ground
of the border
p. 246*

Miscanthus sinensis 'Morning Light'

'Morning Light' miscanthus
Height: 4–5 ft.
Deep pink-bronze flowers in early to midfall
Zones 5–9

Plant by itself or in groups, with woody or evergreen shrubs
p. 246

Miscanthus sinensis 'Purpurascens'

Flame grass
Height: 3–4 ft.
Compact; fall foliage color holds into winter
Zones 4–8

Plant alongside shrubs with bright fall foliage
p. 247

**Miscanthus
sinensis
'Silberfeder'**

*'Silver Feather'
miscanthus*
Height: 6–9 ft.
Cascading foliage
and flowers;
summer-blooming
Zones 5–9

Plant with
evergreen shrubs,
near a pool or pond
p. 247

**Miscanthus
sinensis 'Undine'**

*'Undine'
miscanthus*
Height: 4 ft.
Slender, compact
grass; *warm fall
color*
Zones 5–9

Good size for
mixed border
p. 248

**Miscanthus
sinensis
'Variegatus'**

*Variegated
miscanthus
Height: 6–9 ft.
Abundant pink
flowers 1–2 ft.
above foliage in
early fall
Zones 6–9*

*Tolerates shade
p. 248*

**Miscanthus
sinensis 'Zebrinus'**

*Zebra grass
Height: 6–8 ft.
Wide-arching
clumps may need
support
Zones 6–9*

*Popular at water's
edge
p. 248*

Miscanthus transmorrisonensis

Evergreen miscanthus
Height: 3–4 ft.
Spring-blooming in mild climates, early to midsummer in cool climates
Zones 7–10

Fine specimen
p. 249

Molinia caerulea 'Heidebraut'

'Heather Bride' moor grass
Height: 2–3 ft.
Compact green tufts with abundant, tall flower stalks
Zones 5–8

Bloom adds vertical line to garden
p. 250

| *Molinia caerulea* ssp. *litorialis* | Tall moor grass Height: 2–3 ft. Flowers rise 6–9 ft. above low, dense tufts in summer Zones 5–8 | Use in border or naturalistic garden p. 250 |

| *Molinia caerulea* ssp. *litorialis* 'Skyracer' | 'Skyracer' tall moor grass Height: 2–3 ft. One of the tallest in bloom; straight flower stems rise 7–8 ft. Zones 5–8 | Adds architectural accent p. 250 |

Muhlenbergia dumosa

*Bamboo muhly
Height: 3–9 ft.
Cool-season
perennial; arching
foliage resembles
fine bamboo
Zones 8–10*

*Heat- and drought-
tolerant
p. 251*

Muhlenbergia pubescens

*Soft blue Mexican
muhly
Height: 8–12 in.
Low-mounding
perennial; downy
evergreen foliage;
gray-blue flowers
Zones 9–10*

*Plant in groups or
singly
p. 252*

Muhlenbergia rigens

*Deer grass
Height: 2–4 ft.
Western cool-
season native;
green foliage holds
color through
summer
Zones 7–9*

*Use in naturalistic
dry garden, or as
hillside ground
cover
p. 253*

Oryzopsis hymenoides

*Indian rice grass
Height: 12–30 in.
Cool-season tufted
grass; delicate
panicles open in
spring
Zones 7–10*

*Good in a
xeriscape with
perennials and
silver-foliaged
plants
p. 254*

Panicum virgatum   *Switch grass*   *Tolerates wet and*
                        Height: 3–7 ft.   *dry sites*
                        Good fall color;   *p. 256*
                        flowers held high
                        above leaves in
                        summer
                        Zones 5–9

Panicum virgatum   *'Cloud Nine'*   *Plant in a meadow,*
'Cloud Nine'   *switch grass*   *groupings*
                        Height: 4–6 ft.   *p. 256*
                        Medium-tall
                        clumping perennial;
                        flowers persist into
                        winter
                        Zones 5–9

Panicum virgatum   'Haense Herms' red   Plant in masses,
'Haense Herms'   switch grass   borders
                         Height: 3–4 ft.   p. 256
                         Flowers and foliage
                         suffused with red in
                         early autumn
                         Zones 5–9

Panicum virgatum   'Heavy Metal'   Outstanding
'Heavy Metal'   switch grass   mixed-border
                         Height: 3–5 ft.   plant; maintains
                         Columnar form;   form in the winter
                         unusual blue-gray   garden
                         foliage turns yellow   p. 257
                         in fall
                         Zones 4–9

Panicum virgatum   'Red Rays' red   Plant in the mixed
'Rotstrahlbusch'   switch grass   border; in groupings
                            Height: 3–4 ft.   or drifts
                            Excellent red fall   p. 257
                            foliage
                            Zones 5–9

Panicum virgatum   'Squaw' switch   Partner with warm-
'Squaw'   grass   or cool-season
                            Height: 3–4 ft.   grasses or shrubs
                            Loose habit;   with good fall color
                            purple-red leaves   p. 257
                            by late summer
                            Zones 4–9

Pennisetum alopecuroides 'Cassian'

'Cassian' fountain grass
Height: 12–24 in.
Dwarf cultivar; soft flower spikes reach 2 ft. high
Zones 4–9

Perfect for the front of the border
p. 258

Pennisetum alopecuroides 'Moudry'

Black-flowered fountain grass
Height: 2–3 ft.
Unusual black flowers; variable bloomer; invasive in mild climates
Zones 7–9

Shade-tolerant p. 259

| **Pennisetum macrostachyum 'Burgundy Giant'** | 'Burgundy Giant' fountain grass Height: 4–5 ft. Flowers in midsummer; grow as annual in cold climates Zones 9–10 | Combine with other grasses, shrubs, and perennials in a protected site p. 259 |

| **Pennisetum orientale** | Oriental fountain grass Height: 1–2 ft. Early blooming; grow as annual in cold climates Zones 7–9 | Beautiful near water, as a specimen or in a group p. 260 |

Pennisetum setaceum 'Rubrum'

Crimson fountain grass
Height: 2–3 ft.
Tender cultivar; mounding fine-textured burgundy foliage
Zones 9–10

Grow as annual in cold climates
p. 261

Pennisetum villosum

Feathertop
Height: 24–30 in.
Tender perennial; fluffy foxtails all summer; can be a pest in Midwest and South
Zones 8–9

Good for coastal gardens
p. 261

| **Phalaris arundinacea 'Feesey'** | 'Feesey' ribbon grass Height: 2–3 ft. Fine leaves blush pink in spring; showy white flowers in summer Zones 4–9 | Invasive; grow as ground cover or provide barriers p. 262 |

| **Phalaris arundinacea 'Picta'** | Ribbon grass Height: 2–4 ft. Warm-season running grass; invasive in all but very dry gardens Zones 4–9 | Grow as ground cover or as aquatic in shallow water p. 262 |

Phormium tenax

*New Zealand flax
Height: 8–9 ft.
Large grasslike
plant with 5-in.-
wide spear-shaped
leaves
Zones 8–10*

*Tall stalks of
reddish flowers in
summer
p. 263*

**Phyllostachys
aureosulcata**

*Yellow groove
bamboo
Height: 15–20 ft.
Highly invasive
plant will form
groves
Zones 6–10*

*Handsome screen
when contained
p. 264*

Phyllostachys nigra

Black bamboo
Height: 10–25 ft.
Striking culms ideal
for Japanese garden
Zones 7–10

Invasive; grow in
containers
p. 264

Rhynchelytrum repens

Natal grass
Height: 1–4 ft.
Short-lived
clumping perennial;
long bloom time
Zones 9–10

Rampant self-sower
in warm climates
p. 266

Sasa veitchii

Silver-edge bamboo
Height: 2–3 ft.
Low-spreading,
broad-leaved
bamboo; holds
color all winter
Zones 7–10

Ground cover for
shade or traditional
Japanese garden
p. 268

***Schizachyrium
scoparium***

Little bluestem
Height: 2–3 ft.
Prairie native;
slender green
foliage in summer
Zones 3–9

Naturalistic
plantings, large-
scale ground cover,
or in the mixed
border
p. 269

Semiarundinaria murielae

*Running bamboo
Height: 10–15 ft.
Tall, dense, slow-
spreading bamboo;
clump creates
weeping-willow
effect
Zones 7–10*

*Trouble-free; use as
screen
p. 272*

Sesleria autumnalis

*Autumn moor
grass
Height: 18 in.
Evergreen, shade-
tolerant
Zones 5–9*

*Plant in sweeps
p. 273*

Sesleria heufleriana

*Green moor grass
Height: 12–18 in.
Young leaves
powdered with
white
Zones 5–9*

*Tough plant for
rock gardens
p. 273*

Sorghastrum nutans

*Indian grass
Height: 3–8 ft
Perennial tallgrass
prairie native; good
fall and winter
color
Zones 4–9*

*Use as accent, in
border, or as screen
p. 274*

***Sorghastrum nutans* 'Sioux Blue'**	*'Sioux Blue' Indian grass* *Height: 3–5 ft.* *Silvery blue cultivar with very erect habit* *Zones 4–9*	*Use as single specimen or plant as mass* *p. 275*

Spartina pectinata	*Prairie cord grass* *Height: 4–6 ft.* *Perennial running grass with arching sharp-edged leaves* *Zones 4–9*	*Thrives along water; more restrained in dry soil* *p. 275*

Spodiopogon sibiricus

*Frost grass
Height: 2–3 ft.
Slow-spreading;
bamboolike foliage
turns colorful in
fall; pretty flowers
in late summer
Zones 5–9*

*Plant as specimen
or in masses in sun
or shade
p. 276*

Sporobolus heterolepsis

*Prairie dropseed
Height: 18–30 in.
Mounding
perennial grass;
fine leaves turn
orange and gold in
fall
Zones 4–8*

*Easy-care plant
anywhere in the
garden
p. 277*

Stipa gigantea

*Giant feather grass
Height: 2–3 ft.
Cool-season
perennial flowers
late spring to early
summer
Zones 7–9*

*Specimen,
naturalized
planting
p. 279*

**Stipa tenuissima
'Pony Tails'**

'Pony Tails'
Mexican feather
grass
Height: 12–18 in.
Silky flowers from
late spring through
fall
Zones 7–10

Aggressive self-
sower; plant in a
naturalized
meadow
p. 280

Tripsicum dactyloides

Gama grass
Height: 6–10 ft.
Striking male and
female flowers
Zones 4–9

Thrives near water,
in shade
p. 281

Typha latifolia

Cattail
Height: 3–5 ft.
Perennial rushlike
plant for wet sites;
velvety brown
pokers persist
through fall
Zones 4–9

Colonizes rapidly
around and in
shallow water
p. 282

Uniola paniculata   *Sea oats*
                        Height: 3–8 ft.
                        Perennial coastal
                        native; spreads
                        slowly by creeping
                        rhizomes
                        Zones 7–10

Needs sandy soil;
sensitive to foot
traffic
p. 283

Vetiveria   *Vetiver*
zizanioides   *Height: 4–10 ft.*
                        Perennial warm-
                        season grass;
                        evergreen in frost-
                        free climates
                        Zones 9–10

Native to wet
places but tolerates
drought
p. 284

Yucca filamentosa

*Bear grass
Height: 2–3 ft.
Evergreen perennial
with swordlike
leaves and very
showy flowers in
June
Zones 5–10*

*Grow in average to
dry soils; requires
little care*
p. 284

Zea mays

*Ornamental corn
Height: 3–15 ft.
Various cultivars
offer colorful leaves
and decorative ears
Zones 4–9*

*Grow as a hedge or
background
planting*
p. 286

Encyclopedia of Grasses

The plants described in this section are organized alphabetically by genus. A short description of the genus is followed by individual entries for featured species and cultivars. These entries pack a lot of information into a small space. We hope they will be easy to follow. Here are a few comments to help you make the best use of them.

Names

Plant taxonomists are continually reclassifying plants and renaming the groupings to which the plants are assigned, making any book outdated almost before it appears. This is particularly true of grasses. We have tried to use names and classifications current at the time of writing, but have included synonyms by which many nurseries (and taxonomists) may still identify the plant.

Characteristics

The beginning of each entry provides certain basic information about the plant for quick reference, including its common names, its hardiness zone rating, and its height and spread. In addition, we have used abbreviations to indicate whether the plant is an annual (A), perennial (P), or perennial grown as an annual (PGA). Clump-forming grasses (Cl) are distinguished from running grasses (R); and warm-season grasses (W) from cold-season grasses (C), a distinction drawn only for plants in the grass family (Gramineae). Some grasses are neither clumping nor running, and their habits are discussed in the text.

Achnatherum

Ak-nath´er-um

Gramineae. Grass family

Cool-season perennial grasses with loose, arching foliage and soft spears of flowers. As with many grasses, the botanical name of this genus and its species is debated by taxonomists. Some consider the grasses of this Eurasian genus a part of the genus *Stipa*, which includes related needle grasses and spear grasses of North America, South America, Europe, Asia, and Australia.

■ *calamagrostis* *p. 116*
(Stipa calamagrostis)
Silver spear grass, reed grass, silver spike grass
Zones 6–9. P/Cl/C
Height: 18–36 in. Spread: 24 in. or more

A mid-height clumping grass of fine texture with beautiful fluffy flower heads. The narrow plumes of flowers are held about 6 in. above the leaves on arching stems that follow the graceful sweep of the foliage. The flower heads have a silky, purplish sheen when newly emerged in June and change to glistening silvery white and finally to deep tan. Flowers persist through winter. Leaves turn amber in fall, then lighten to tan in winter. In mild-winter climates, the foliage may retain some green through most of the year.

The graceful, abundant flowers at a moderate height make silver spike grass an asset in borders, groups, or naturalistic plantings, where it can hold its own even with aggressive perennials such as pink evening primrose *(Oenothera speciosa)*. It is also attractive along streams or ponds. For an ethereal combination, plant lady's-mantle around the feet of this grass and wait for a heavy dew. The soft plumes of grass flowers collect droplets of dew like a fine silver net, while the wide, pleated lady's-mantle leaves beneath are spangled with larger droplets.

How to Grow

Full or part sun; water regularly for best growth. Thrives in a wide range of soils, from clay to loam. Spreads moderately in loose, moist soil; heavy or dry soils keep it in a clump. Originally from the cool mountains of Europe, this grass languishes in hot, dry climates. Cut back in early spring. Divide in spring or throughout growing season. Flowers are good in fresh or dried bouquets and swags.

Acorus

Uh-kor´us

Araceae. Arum family

Perennial plants of marshes and wetlands, which sprout fans of irislike leaves from fleshy rhizomes. The plants thrive in wet soil, but they adapt to life in average garden soil, and some also flourish in containers. The genus includes only two species, from Europe, Asia, and the Far East. The roots of *Acorus calamus,* or sweet flag, were brought to England and later to America as part of the early pharmacopeia, and today this plant can be found growing thickly along moats and lakes around old British castles and in wet places from Nova Scotia to Minnesota, south to Kansas and Louisiana.

■ *calamus*

Sweet flag

Zones 4–10. P/R

Height: 24–36 in. Spread: 18–24 in. or more

This slender-leaved plant looks like an iris or a big grass, but it's really a relative of the classic calla lily and the familiar wildflower, Jack-in-the-pulpit, which you can see by the club-shaped flowering spadix, typical of the arums. Sweet flag is beautiful along the water's edge, where its tall, erect 1-in.-wide leaves rustle and move in the wind. Wild stock can reach 6 ft. tall, but most nursery plants top out at 3 ft. or less. The odd but sweetly fragrant flowers stick out from the leaf stems at 45° angles. The linear form of the plants is a good foil for the enormous rounded leaves of rodgersia or gunnera. The slim blades also look good when combined with the arrowhead leaves of blue-flowered pickerelweed.

The thick, long, branching roots are pungently aromatic; British aristocrats once powdered their wigs with scented powder made from them. The roots have also been used as flavoring, in candy, or distilled in oil for perfume, as well as a medicinal remedy. (The FDA disapproved medicinal use after tests showed it to be carcinogenic.) The leaves are nicely fragrant and in the days of chamber pots and infrequent bathing were used as a "strewing herb," spread on floors to create a pleasant scent.

How to Grow

Full sun to light shade. Boggy or moist soil high in organic matter. Will also tolerate standing water of several inches' depth, and will thrive in garden soil of average moistness. Best at water's edge, where it spreads at a moderate pace. Divide in spring or fall, digging up a piece of rhizome and replanting.

■ *calamus* 'Variegatus'   *p. 116*
Variegated sweet flag
Zones 5–10. P/R
Height: 24–36 in. Spread: 12 in. or more
   A striking, boldly striped version of sweet flag, this cultivar looks yellow at a distance. Its creamy white to yellow stripes make it an attention-getter in the garden; use it as an accent among green-foliaged plants, or with blue or white Siberian or Japanese irises or glowing yellow monkey flower (*Mimulus* spp.). Leaves are about 1 in. wide.

How to Grow
Like *A. calamus.* Branching, creeping rhizomes spread more slowly than the species.

■ *gramineus*
Japanese sweet flag
Zones 7–9. P/R
Height: 6–12 in. Spread: 8 in. or more
   A downscaled version of sweet flag, with narrow leaves like thick, lush grass. The species reaches 12 in. tall, but dwarf cultivars as short as 5 in. are also available. The glossy $1/_2$-in.-wide leaves are wonderfully fragrant, which makes this plant a perfect choice for edging walkways or as a ground cover, where foot traffic will release the fragrance. You can even use it in place of lawn grass in small areas. Its spreading roots also find a home among rocks, such as in an informal garden or between stepping-stones or along a pool edging. The soil stays cool and moist beneath the rocks, and the swords of leaves are a good contrast in line and texture.

How to Grow
Sun or part sun. Moist or well-watered soil; perfect for the edges of ponds or other water features, where it will thrive in wet soil. Also makes a good container plant, if frequently watered. Leaf tips die back when water is scarce. Gradually spreads into a seamless turf. Propagate by division in spring or fall. Spider mites may web the undersides of the lush foliage, causing the upper sides to become mottled and sickly; wash off the pests with a blast of water from the garden hose or cut back the leaves to ground level and let them regrow.

■ *gramineus* 'Ogon'   *p. 117*
Golden variegated Japanese sweet flag
Zones 6–9. P/R
Height: 10 in. Spread: 12 in. or more
   Beautiful golden yellow, fine-textured foliage produced in abundance has a casual attitude, arching in various directions

like a tousled head of hair. Its color will light up a partly shady spot or draw attention to a pond or pool. Plant at a bend in a path to catch the eye and draw the feet onward. If you plant it where late afternoon sun can shine through the foliage, the plant will almost glow with warm color. Try golden variegated sweet flag in a mass planting. The leaves are only $1/8$–$1/4$ in. wide, which keeps even a large planting from becoming an overpowering presence.

How to Grow
Sun or part sun. Flourishes in moist soil, but will also grow well in garden soil of average moisture. A good container plant. Well suited for planting near water.

■ *gramineus* 'Variegatus'
Variegated Japanese sweet flag
Zones 7–9. P/R
Height: 6–12 in. Spread: 6 in. or more
   This small but eye-catching cultivar grows in tufts of creamy white-striped fine-leaved foliage. Plant as individual accents or in a mass. (They spread slowly, so plant close together.) Try the cool green-white of variegated sweet flag with a stand of high-voltage red cardinal flower, or use this grasslike plant in the foreground of a group of waterside plants of similar upright habit but coarser texture and greater stature.

How to Grow
Light shade. Flourishes in moist soil, but will also grow in garden soil of average moisture. Excellent along water.

Agropyron

Ag-roe-py´run
Gramineae. Grass family

Cool-season perennial grasses of clumping habit, with tufts of fine-textured foliage. Most often used for hay, pasture, or lawn grass, but also includes outstanding ornamentals, as well as one of the worst garden pests, quack grass *(Agropyron repens)*. The genus is closely related to wheat *(Triticum aestivum)*, and some botanists believe that wheat may have developed as a hybrid with this genus. (The name *Agropyron* is from the Greek *agrios,* wild, and *puros,* wheat.) About 40 species, native to and widely distributed throughout the Northern and Southern Hemispheres.

■ *magellanicum* *p. 117*
(Elymus magellanicus)
Blue Magellan grass
Zones 5–8. P/Cl/C
Height: 12–18 in. Spread: 12–18 in.

Dense, spiky tufts are an ethereal gray-blue, the color of the best blue spruces. The $\frac{1}{4}$–$\frac{1}{2}$-in.-wide leaves are similar in appearance to blue Lyme grass *(Elymus arenarius* 'Glaucus'), but the clumping plant lacks the rampant invasive tendencies of that species. Flowers look like heads of wheat and are appealing in arrangements. The seed heads ripen to tan, but the grass may stay evergreen, especially in mild-winter climates. Be careful working around Magellan grass; its leaves can be sharp and prickly.

The small tufts are easy to incorporate with flowering perennials. The gray-blue color is beautiful with pink flowers such as dianthus, and it makes yellow and white flowers stand out with extra dash. Hot pink and magenta are cooled by the blue grass, which works well when planted in groups as a transition between colors. Also a good companion for red-leaved barberries.

The cultivar 'Longwood' is shorter than the species (to 8 in.) with equally striking foliage that appears light blue to gray-green depending on your vantage point.

How to Grow

Full sun. Moist, well-drained soil. Thrives in coastal conditions, even when exposed to salt spray. Not suited for hot, humid conditions; not drought-tolerant. Cut back once a year to encourage new, brightly colored growth.

Ammophila

Uh-moh´fill-uh
Gramineae. Grass family
Erect, perennial grasses of sandy shores, with long, tough, sharp-pointed leaves and far-reaching rhizomatous roots. Includes only four species.

■ *breviligulata*   *p. 118*
American beach grass
Zones 4–7. P/R/W
Height: 24–36 in. Spread: 36 in. or more
Long, thin, gray-green leaves rise from tough rhizomatous roots that spread widely in sandy soil. Plants grow in loose colonies, throwing up new shoots far from the mother plant. Leaf blades are tipped by dangerously sharp points that are a threat to the eyes of dogs, children, and others. Blooms in late July or August, with long, narrow, soft-textured spikes resembling golden tan pipe cleaners. Flowers persist until their stems break from coastal winds.

In its native range, the East Coast and the Great Lakes, American beach grass is useful in home landscapes for covering a steep bank because it spreads fast and needs no maintenance. It also makes a good low-maintenance ground cover for a naturalistic yard, where it can be combined beautifully with native lupines in shades of blue, white, and yellow. Sparrows nest in the hillocky clumps.

The introduced European species, *Ammophila arenaria* (European beach grass), was once a favorite for dune stabilization but has proved so invasive on the West Coast that it is listed by the California Native Plant Society as one of the most problematic weeds. It threatens coastal sand dune systems by outcompeting native dune plants and interfering with the natural dynamics of dune systems. On the Atlantic Coast, it greatly alters beach profiles and subsequently changes the impact and effect of storms on the coastline.

How to Grow
Full sun or part sun. Sand or sandy soil. If planting in pure sand, set out new divisions at least 10 in. deep, where the sand feels moist. The buried roots will soon take hold and send up new shoots. Propagate by division in spring or fall.

Andropogon

an-dro-po´gun
Gramineae. Grass family
Perennial, warm-season grasses of varying habit, some tall

and clumping, others short and creeping. Includes one of the main grasses of the American tallgrass prairie. About 200 species, native to temperate and tropical regions throughout the world.

■ *gerardii* *p. 118*
Big bluestem, turkeyfoot, turkey claw, beardgrass, bluejoint
Zones 4–9. P/Cl/W
Height: 48–96 in. Spread: 24 in. or more

One of the dominant grasses of the American tallgrass prairie that once covered millions of acres, big bluestem is being discovered by gardeners for its ornamental effects and undemanding attitude. It is a willowy grass of great height, but most of its foliage stays in an erect, slightly arching clump of gently curling leaves that usually reaches about 2–3 ft. tall. Its soft, ¼-in.-wide foliage is lead-gray to bluish green when it emerges in spring; plants vary in their blueness when young, as well as in their retention of the color as they mature, with most turning green. At bloom time in late summer and early autumn, the flowering stems rise to the height of a person or taller. The distinctive 3-angled flowers look like a turkey foot jutting off the top of the skinny, gangly stems. The plant is beautiful in fall, when it takes on warm tan, bronze, and crimson hues. The colors are softened in winter to warm russeted tan with glints of red and bronze; the foliage persists through winter although the seed heads soon shatter.

This clumping plant is a beauty in prairie plantings or in groups of grasses. It's also a treasure in the mixed border. Despite its height, you can place it in the midground of the border as well as the back because its tall flowering stems are not thick with leaves. The plant has an almost see-through quality, like the flowering *Verbena bonariensis;* in fact, the two make a great combination of purple and russet. The clustered spikes of perennial Maximilian sunflower and the drooping yellow petals of prairie coneflower are good partners, as are fall asters in shades of blue and pink.

'Roundtree' has an erect, upright habit of growth and is somewhat smaller in stature than the species, reaching 6 ft. tall under average conditions. It comes into bloom earlier, a good attribute for gardeners with shorter growing seasons. 'The Blues' is another erect-growing cultivar with excellent blue-gray color and vertical line. Both are beautiful with pink astilbe.

How to Grow
Full sun. Average garden soil, including clay. Young plants may seem slow to grow, but they are busy establishing extensive root systems that will be able to withstand considerable drought after three years or longer in the garden. Big bluestem tolerates high summer heat and thrives in humidity as well as dryness. In fertile soil, with abundant rain, the plants can reach 10 ft. tall; under less favorable conditions, the plants are more frugal in their growth and may top out at 4–6 ft. Cut back in early spring. Self-sows readily in ideal conditions. Propagate by division or seed in spring. Use 15 pounds of seed per acre when planting a large area in grass alone or 10 pounds per acre if including flowers and other plants.

■ *saccharoides* *p. 119*
(*Bothriochla saccharoides*)
Silver bluestem, silver beardgrass
Zones 5–9. P/Cl/W
Height: 12–18 in. Spread: 12 in. or more
Native to the American Southwest, silver bluestem forms thick tufts of fine leaf blades that sprout delightful little puffs of silvery white seed heads at the tops of slim, erect, 2–3-ft. flowering stems. In fall, the grass turns rich colors of purple to pumpkin orange that mellow a bit during the dormant season but still hold enough color to be a welcome sight in the winter. Once used for hay, silver bluestem is a beautiful addition to the garden, especially when naturalized in a meadow or on a slope where the sun can backlight the fluffy hairs of the eye-catching seed heads.

How to Grow
Full sun. Average garden soil. Cut back in early spring. Propagate by seed or division.

Anthoxanthum

an-tho-zan´thum

Gramineae. Grass family

Annual or perennial cool-season grasses with fairly short tufts of soft, fine-textured leaves that have a wonderful aromatic fragrance. About six species native to Eurasia and North Africa. The species below is naturalized in the eastern United States and along the Pacific Coast.

■ *odoratum*

Sweet vernal grass

Zones 5–10. P/Cl/C

Height: 12–24 in. Spread: 6 in. or more

This cool-season clumping perennial grass smells like fresh-cut clover when its leaves are crushed or crumpled. The dense, spiky-looking but soft tufts stay about 6 in. tall, with 12–18-in. flowering stems emerging to spray out over the plant. The grass is evergreen, but the slender spikes of flowers bloom in spring and soon dry to golden brown. You can clip them off or cut back the grass for a neater look.

Sweet vernal grass is not particularly showy, but it is nice when planted in grassy footpaths, spilling onto pathways, or in a lawn area, where its scent can be enjoyed as the leaves are bruised by foot traffic. Kids and adults alike enjoy pulling a sweet-tasting flowering stem to nibble. You can cut leaves and twist them into small, fragrant knots or wreaths for indoors; they hold their scent for a long time after cutting.

How to Grow

Full sun or part sun. Average garden soil. Plant in light shade in areas with scorching summer sun. May self-sow. Propagate by seed or division.

Aristida

uh-ris´tih-duh

Gramineae. Grass family

Perennial clumping grasses of the American shortgrass prairie. Formerly ignored by horticulturists, the genus includes several decorative species that are valuable in naturalistic landscaping in hot, dry areas such as the desert Southwest.

■ *purpurea* *p. 119*

Purple three-awn

Zones 6–9. P/Cl/C

Height: 12–30 in. Spread: 12 in.

This heat-tolerant perennial grass forms dense but airy-looking tufts of rolled, $\frac{1}{32}$–$\frac{1}{16}$-in.-wide leaves that often curl and twist. The "three awns" of the seed heads have very long, silky hairs that catch the light like spiderweb threads in the sun. The feathery, delicate flowering stems grow 18–30 in. tall, but are often loose and lax. They have a purple sheen that matures to platinum blond above the golden tufts of foliage.

Plant this grass where it can naturalize, which it will do by seeding itself. Keep it away from traffic, and avoid planting it if you have long-haired pets — the bristled seed heads catch on clothing and fur and can become painful irritants as the needlelike awns coil tightly to "plant" the seed in your pants leg or other inappropriate place.

How to Grow
Full sun. Average garden soil. Tolerates drought and heat. Propagate by seed or division in spring. Purple three-awn is a native grass of the American shortgrass prairie, which once covered the west-central United States. Grasses from this area are well adapted to the dry conditions found in the rain shadow of the Rockies; their roots are short and wide-spreading, and the plants typically grow in spaced clumps (bunchgrasses), so that each benefits from as much moisture as possible.

Arrhenatherum
ah-ren-ath´ur-um
Gramineae. Grass family
Perennial grasses of varying habit, including a useful pasture grass for humid regions and an old-fashioned favorite ornamental grass. Includes six species, all native to the Mediterranean region.

■ *elatius* var. *bulbosum* 'Variegatum' *p. 120*
Variegated bulbous oat grass, variegated tuberous oat grass
Zones 4–9. P/R/C
Height: 8–24 in. Spread: 8–12 in.
The ghostly color and short to medium height of this perennial cool-season clumping grass make it a prize in the perennial border. Its narrow leaf blades are about $\frac{1}{8}$–$\frac{1}{4}$ in. wide and look spiky but are soft to the touch. From a distance, the grass glows silvery white; only at close range do you notice the thin green stripe along the center of each leaf. The narrow panicles of flowers, which look like bristly wild oats, emerge in late spring to early summer, but they're not especially decorative, and the grass is not at its best by then.

The luminous tuft of leaves looks great with perennials and bulbs that flower in early to late spring, when oat grass is at its peak. It's also fun to play with foliage effects, such as combining its narrow, spiky form and color with the broader, silver-spangled leaves of lungwort and waterleaf. It's beautiful with blue catmint, especially the taller cultivar 'Six Hills Giant' and with hardy geraniums of all colors. When the grass begins to sprawl and flag in summer, even before blooming, many gardeners cut it back hard and let other plants, such as baby's-breath or perovskia, take its place. If you give it generous water after cutting back, the foliage may sprout anew. When you cut back the clump, note the unusual bulbous nodes from which the grass sprouts, jointed like short vertical strings of children's pop-it beads.

How to Grow
Full sun to part sun. Moist, well-drained soil. Plant in light shade in areas with hot summers. May be infected by the rust virus; immediately cut off and remove any orange-blotched or yellowing foliage. Divide any time of the growing season, giving new starts generous water until they're established.

Arundinaria
A-run-di-nayr´ee-a
Gramineae. Grass family
   Hardy bamboos with spreading rhizomes and leafy upright stems. Flowering is rare; when it occurs, all members of a species flower simultaneously over a large area. About 30 species, native to the Old and New Worlds.

■ *viridistriata* *p. 120*
(now *Pleioblastus viridistriatus*)
Running bamboo, golden bamboo
Zone 4. P/R
Height: 30 in. Spread: indefinite
   The new leaves of this dwarf spreading bamboo are vibrant gold with bright green stripes. It is invasive but less so than other small running bamboos. Useful as a ground cover to control erosion on steep banks or as a tough, low-maintenance cover for areas surrounded by concrete sidewalks or drives. Use it to brighten a shady corner or woodland edge, and try interplanting it with gold or purple crocuses, yellow narcissus, and red or purple tulips. Can be grown in a container on a deck or patio. *A. variegata*, 13 ft. in height, is similar but has white-striped leaves; it runs aggressively and must be confined.

How to Grow

Tolerates shade, but sun makes the leaves a brighter yellow. Ordinary soil and watering. Hardier than formerly acknowledged; tops freeze back, but runners survive. Buy one to start with; you can soon divide it if you want more. Use hand pruners or a string trimmer to mow off old stems in spring.

Arundo

uh-run´doe
Gramineae. Grass family

Tall, perennial, reedlike grasses with broad leaf blades and plumed flowers. About six species, native to tropical and subtropical areas of the Old World.

■ *donax* p. 121
Giant reed, giant cane, carrizo
Zones 6–10. P/R/W
Height: 9–25 ft. Spread: 36 in. or more

Tallest of the ornamental grasses, this species can reach 20 ft. or higher in ideal conditions of moisture and year-round warmth. Garden-grown plants in cold-winter areas usually top out at about 10–12 ft. Giant reed looks like a huge bamboo, with leaves that can reach 3 in. wide and 24 in. long. Large soft flower panicles bloom in fall in mild climates; in cold areas, the plants may not bloom. Giant cane turns beige with the onset of cold weather, and the leaves rattle coarsely in the wind. The thick, jointed stems have been used for thousands of years for homebuilding, lattices, and animal fences in some countries. Split stems are used for reeds in woodwind instruments (sections of stem were also once used for organ pipes in Europe).

In the garden, giant reed is best used as an accent near water, where its gangly height looks most at home. The large clumps expand by rhizomatous roots, which grow fast in mild-winter climates and make giant reed a poor choice for gardeners in such areas. The plant is much less invasive in areas with cold winters, where it can make a fast-growing hedge or windbreak.

How to Grow

Sun. Average garden soil. Moist soil and frequent watering encourages aggressive root growth. Plant in spring. Cut back old foliage in early spring; use woody old stems for plant supports in perennial or vegetable garden. Propagate by division or take cuttings of rhizomes in early spring.

■ *donax* 'Variegata' *p. 121*
Striped giant reed
Zones 8–10. P/R/W
Height: 5–12 ft. Spread: 36 in. or more

This statuesque plant has broad leaves striped with white, cream, or yellow, which give it a golden appearance, especially at the top of the plant. The color turns greener as the leaves age during the season. Under average garden conditions, striped giant reed stays about 5–7 ft. tall. Like the plain green species, plants are taller and more robust in mild-winter areas or when given plenty of moisture. In cold-winter areas, this grass makes a good tall accent in a mixed planting with miscanthus and other large-size grasses. Striped giant reed is evergreen in mild climates, but freezes to beige in cold weather.

How to Grow
Like *Arundo donax.*

Bambusa

Bam-boo´sa. Bamboo
Gramineae. Grass family

Clump-forming bamboos, some with large woody culms. About 100 species, native to tropical and warm climates.

■ *oldhamii p. 122*
Giant timber bamboo
Zone 8. P/Cl
Height: 50–55 ft. Spread: 20 ft.

Truly a giant, it makes a huge green fountain for tropical or Oriental effects. The stems are green, turning yellow, up to 4 in. thick, and make good poles for fencing or other garden structures. The thin, bright green leaves are up to 12 in. long. Use single plants or pairs to mark an impressive entry. Plant with bananas, elephant's-ear, or gingers for a tropical look. This bamboo is a clumper. Another giant timber bamboo, *Phyllostachys bambusoides,* is a runner and will in time form open groves to 45 ft. tall, with 6-in. stems. It is hardier (Zone 7) than *B. oldhamii.*

How to Grow
Full sun. Ordinary soil and watering okay, but grows larger with fertile soil and ample water. One plant is usually enough. For a really big screen to block undesirable views, plant 10–15 ft. apart. To divide old plants, use pick, axe, and saw in spring. The fallen leaves of all bamboos may be considered

litter, or you could think of them as an attractive, weed-suppressive mulch.

Bouteloua

boot-uh-loo´uh

Gramineae. Grass family

These fine-bladed perennial and annual warm-season grasses are mainstays of natural grasslands in North and South America and are still used as pasture and forage grasses. Named after the Bouteloua brothers of Spain, who were among the first to cultivate a native grass for use in gardens, they make a good addition to naturalistic garden plantings because of their interesting flowering spikes. About 50 species, native to the Americas from the central United States to Argentina. All are commonly known as grama grasses.

■ *curtipendula* *p. 122*

Sideoats grama, sideoats gramma

Zones 4–9. P/Cl/W

Height: 24–36 in. Spread: 18 in.

This clumping perennial grass has wonderfully decorative flowers that dangle like a line of little bells from one side of the graceful flowering stems. They're as pretty in a vase as they are in the garden. Plants grow in a dense clump of fine leaves, usually reaching 1–2 ft. tall. The abundant, gently arching flowering spikes emerge in early summer, sprouting a foot or more above the foliage. Native sparrows and other birds feast on the seeds. The stems persist through winter, mellowing to golden yellow after first taking on a purple hue with frost.

This is a beautiful plant for a meadow or prairie garden. Its soft tufts of narrow, $1/8$–$1/4$-in.-wide leaves combine easily with the simple blooms of native wildflowers such as California poppies or mallows. In winter, a mass planting of the standing clumps provides shelter for birds and small mammals. It can also be used as a lawn grass.

How to Grow
Sun. Very tolerant of soil, thriving equally well in poor, sandy soils; heavy clay; or rich, loose loam. Drought-tolerant. Plant seed or divisions in spring. Propagate by seed or division. May self-sow, but unwanted seedlings are easily smothered by mulch. Mow or clip each year to about half its height to remove old seed stems and clean out dead thatch. As a lawn, mow to about 2–4 in.; it will spread densely. Tolerant of foot traffic.

■ *gracilis* *p. 123*
Blue grama grass, blue gramma grass
Zones 3–10. P/Cl/W
Height: 8–24 in. Spread: 6–12 in.
Formerly propagated for use as a pasture grass, blue grama is gaining acceptance as an ornamental thanks to its diminutive size, which makes it easy to use in gardens, and its interesting flower heads, which are tightly bunched into thick little brushes that jut out from the stems at 45° angles. The grass blooms in summer, and seed heads remain decorative for a long time. Like sideoats grama, this grama grass turns purplish with cold weather, then gradually changes to a warm tan for winter. Blue grama also makes a hardy, drought-tolerant lawn grass in arid regions.

How to Grow
Sun. Any soil, except for wet soils or heavy clay. Another tough grama grass, this species will withstand extremes of heat, drought, and cold. It self-sows generously, but since it looks best in mass plantings, that trait is usually not a problem. Plant seed or divisions in spring. Mow large plantings or cut back individual plants in early spring to remove old foliage. Propagate by seed or division. If plants develop "fairy-ring" (center of clump dying out), dig out center, add fresh soil, and insert a few new divisions.

Briza

bri´zuh

Gramineae. Grass family

A widespread genus of annual and perennial grasses with showy panicles of dangling, trembling seed heads that are widely used in dried arrangements. The botanical name is from the Greek *brizein*, to nod. About 20 species, native to Eurasia, the Mediterranean, and other temperate regions, and widely naturalized in North America.

■ *media* *p. 123*
Perennial quaking grass
Zones 4–8. P/Cl/W
Height: 24–36 in. Spread: 12–18 in.

This perennial cool-season grass bears erect panicles of small round seed heads that look almost like dainty white baby's-breath flowers from a distance. The plants form small clumps of soft, $\frac{1}{4}$–$\frac{1}{2}$-in.-wide foliage, usually about 12–18 in. tall. Flowers rise well above the plant, where their charming form can be easily seen. The wiry stems that hold each seed head to the main flowering stem look thin and fragile, but they're surprisingly strong, and the panicles persist for several weeks after flowering in spring. Bright green at first, they soften to warm tan, with the seeds shivering and rattling at the slightest breath of wind.

This is a fine grass for the perennial border because its spangling of dainty flowers bloom in mid- to late spring, accenting their neighbors. Because of the see-through quality of the flowers, you can plant it in the foreground or middle without obscuring other plants. It's also good in masses or meadow plantings.

Annual quaking grass *(B. maxima)* is a smaller plant, its seed heads large, flattened, pointed ovals that hang like pendants from very thin, wiry stems. This easy-to-grow plant is appealing in the garden (sow seed where plants are to grow) and its seed heads are long-lasting in dried bouquets. Let them dry to tan on the plant before cutting, or they'll retain a green color.

How to Grow

Full sun. Average soil. Easy to grow. Cut back and water well after blooms shatter to encourage fresh growth. Plant divisions in spring, or in fall in mild-winter climates. Propagate by division.

Buchloe

boo-clo′ee
Gramineae. Grass family
  This genus includes only a single species, the perennial, stoloniferous buffalo grass native to the Great Plains of North America.

■ *dactyloides* *p. 124*
Buffalo grass, buffalo reed grass
Zones 3–9. P/R/W
Height: 4–6 in. Spread: 6 in. or more
  Buffalo grass is perfect for those who hate mowing lawns: it never gets any taller than a few inches, and it spreads to form a fine-textured, gray-green turf. Flowers are short and not a distraction. Unfortunately, the curling leaf blades turn dull beige with cold weather and stay that way until late spring. Many prefer it naturalized rather than mown. The stoloniferous roots are superb at holding soil, making this plant an excellent choice for ground cover on a slope. Lark sparrows, horned larks, and other birds appreciate the seeds.

How to Grow
Full sun. Any soil. Tolerates drought but not wet soil. Plant seeds thickly in pots (they're slow to sprout), or set out divisions in spring. Plugs are available for planting large areas; plant these 4-in. sections about 24 in. apart. This is a tough plant that actually does better in poor soils than in fertile ones. It is slow to spread — a new lawn of buffalo grass may look patchy for its first couple of years. Water very deeply, to 1 ft., every month for the first growing season. Once the grass is established, the runners expand quickly to knit a thick turf. Avoid overwatering once established; abundant moisture increases the height of the plants. Keep buffalo grass away from perennial borders, where its stolons may invade.

Calamagrostis

kal-uh-muh-grahs′tis
Gramineae. Grass family
  Annual or perennial grasses that form large erect clumps with tall, fairly narrow plumes of flowers. Some are important forage grasses, especially in the West. The botanical name refers to their resemblance to reeds: from the Greek *kalamos*, a reed, and *agrostis*, a kind of grass. About 250 species, native to the temperate zones.

■ *acutiflora* 'Karl Foerster' *p. 124*
(C. × *acutiflora* 'Karl Foerster')
'Karl Foerster' feather reed grass
Zones 5–9. P/Cl/C
Height: 5–6 ft. Spread: 24 in.

A strongly vertical plant that makes an exclamation point in the garden, it provides good contrast to low-mounded perennials or shrubs. Makes a clump of very slender, wiry leaves 3 ft. long, with much taller flower stalks spiking up through the center of the clump. The flowers appear in June; the seed heads, slim as pipe cleaners, look pretty all summer and fall as they turn from gold to silver. Leave it untouched at the end of the season; this grass is strong enough to weather the vagaries of winter. 'Sierra', another fine upright cultivar, turns a rich, warm golden brown in late summer.

How to Grow
Full or part sun. Ordinary to poor soil. Tolerates either wet or dry conditions. Divide and plant in spring or late summer. Cut back in early spring.

■ *acutiflora* 'Stricta' *p. 125*
(*Calamagrostis acutiflora* var. *stricta*)
Feather reed grass
Zones 5–9. P/Cl/C
Height: 5–7 ft. Spread: 24 in.

An outstanding grass for the border, for specimen use, or for a mixed grass grouping, this beautiful plant forms dense, 2-ft.-tall clumps of $1/4$–$1/2$-in.-wide leaves, with flowering stems rising stiff and straight from the middle of the plants to create a dense vertical column. The flowering stems rise 3–4 ft. above the foliage and are topped by airy golden plumes, wider and more open than those of *C. a.* 'Karl Foerster'. 'Stricta' blooms in May to June, like a cool-season grass, but it is often evergreen or nearly so in mild-winter climates, where it may refuse to bloom regularly. In cold areas, the foliage ripens to tawny golden orange and persists throughout winter, making a beautiful accent, especially in snow.

The strong vertical line and stature of feather reed grass make it a good plant for the back of the border, where it can be fronted by yarrows, marguerites, shastas and other daisies, and other perennials of loose or mounded habit.

How to Grow
Full sun. Moist soil. Thrives in clay soils. Plant divisions in spring, or in spring or fall in mild-winter climates. Cut back in early spring. Propagate by division.

■ *brachytricha*
(C. arundinacea var. *brachytricha)*
Korean feather reed grass, fall-blooming feather reed grass
Zones 4–9. P/Cl/W
Height: 3–4 ft. Spread: 24–36 in.

At the end of the gardening season, the soft white plumes of Korean feather reed grass spill over boltonias, asters, *Sedum spectabile,* and the last of the garden flowers. This clumping perennial grass is a warm-season grower that forms 18–24-in.-tall mounds of foliage in spring and summer. A wealth of feathery flowers arise at the end of summer for a grand finale. The smoky purple blooms mature to pale beige, while the foliage takes on the color of ripe wheat. The flowers are much fatter and fluffier than the usual narrow spikes of the other feather reed grasses, and the whole plant has a more casual, arching attitude.

How to Grow

Full sun to part sun and light shade. Moist soil. Plant in light shade in hot-summer regions. Water generously during dry weather. Plant divisions in spring. Cut back in early spring. Propagate by division in early spring or fall.

■ *nutkaensis* *p. 125*
Pacific reed grass
Zones 8–9. P/Cl/C
Height: 2–4 ft. Spread: 12–18 in.

West Coast hikers may encounter this native species in coastal meadows along the Pacific, where the shaggy clumps may cover a large area. A cool-season perennial, it thrusts up pointed spears of $\frac{1}{2}$–$\frac{3}{4}$-in.-wide leaves in a dense tuft. Panicles of early to mid-spring-blooming flowers stand 1–2 ft. above the foliage and soon turn from purplish to warm tan.

This is not a grass for the garden, but it does make a good ground cover or low-maintenance planting in coastal and dry-summer areas. It is extremely tolerant of summer drought and thrives in the "serpentine" soils of the West Coast, where natural minerals in the green rock known as serpentine discourage the growth of many plants. This is the dominant native bunchgrass under Monterey pines in Pebble Beach and on the Monterey Peninsula in California. Pacific reed grass also flourishes in the windy, salt-spray extremes of coastal landscapes, where it can be used as a luxuriant mass on steep banks or combined with shrubs such as Santa Barbara ceanothus *(Ceanothus impressus).*

How to Grow

Full sun to partial shade. Thrives in a wide range of soils, from deep, moist soil to clay to rock, and including serpentine. Plant divisions any time from early spring to fall. Cut back in late fall to make way for fresh winter growth. It's easiest to propagate by division, although the plants may occasionally self-sow. Best established by planting nursery-grown plugs, which are about $1\frac{1}{2}$ in. across and 4–6 in. deep.

Carex

care´ex
Cyperaceae. Sedge family
   A huge genus of grasslike perennials, most forming tufts or clumps of slender leaves. All sedges bear clusters of separate male and female flowers on solid, 3-sided stalks. More than 1,000 species, found worldwide but especially in cool, wet climates.

■ *buchananii* *p. 126*
Leatherleaf sedge
Zone 6. P/Cl
Height: 2 ft. Spread: 1 ft.
   Making an airy tuft of shiny cinnamon-colored foliage, the fine delicate leaves arch gracefully and curl at the tips. Leatherleaf sedge offers relief from the green that dominates all gardens, but it also complements blue, white, or reddish brown plants. Combine it with silver-leaved thyme and yellow primroses for winter and spring. It rarely flowers.

How to Grow
Part sun or shade. Ordinary or better soil. Space 1 ft. apart for mass plantings. Divide in spring. Cut foliage back in late fall or early spring. In cold climates, grow one in a container and bring it indoors to a sunny window for the winter.

■ *comans* *p. 126*
(*Carex comans* 'Stricta'; *C. albula*; *C. vilmorinii*)
New Zealand hair sedge
Zones 7–9. P/Cl
Height: 12–24 in. or larger. Spread: 12–18 in.
   This common weed of New Zealand pastures is one of the most beautiful ornamental grasses for the garden. Its exceptionally fine-textured leaves spill into dense tussocks that look like a mop of shining, light green hair. Natural variations in color and habit frequently occur, but all forms of the plant are attractive, whether the leaves are green, brownish, or whitish green. A close look will show that the leaves are rolled almost cylindrically. The plant is often nonflowering.

This sedge can tolerate cold as low as −10°F; if you're a Zone 6 gardener, it's worth chancing it.

New Zealand hair sedge thrives in very moist soil and is perfect along water, where its flowing mane of foliage can be reflected for double the glory. Try it with the contrasting vertical spears of statuesque Japanese iris, or let it be the star of the moist garden, rising from a carpet of blue forget-me-nots or golden moneywort. It is also a solo performer in a large clay pot, where its fine leaves can drape over the side.

The cultivar 'Bronze' looks like a miniature version of the species (growing to 12 in.), but it stays brown year-round, and it isn't quite as flowing. Once you get over the initial "dead-plant" look, you'll find the unusual color combines well with pink flowers or with purple-leaved shrubs such as smokebush. Interesting to grow not only for its own merits, but as a practical joke on garden visitors.

How to Grow
Full sun to part sun. Plant in shade if summers are hot and dry. Thrives in moist soil but also does well in average garden soil. With plenty of moisture, the leaves of some forms can reach 5 ft. or longer. Plant divisions in the spring or sow seeds thickly in pots or a nursery bed. If foliage needs neatening, clip it back in a long crew cut, about 4–5 in. from ground level. Propagate by division; if seed heads develop, the plant may self-sow.

■ *elata* 'Bowles' Golden'
(*Carex elata* 'Aurea'; *C. acuta; C. flava; C. stricta* 'Bowles' Golden')
Bowles' golden sedge, golden sedge
Zones 5–9. P/Cl
Height: 24–36 in. Spread: 24–36 in.

Like a patch of warm sunshine, this golden clump of gently arching foliage lights up the edge of any water garden. The $1/8$–$1/2$-in.-wide leaves are sunny yellow with green edges in spring, deepening to a greener hue by late summer. The plant flowers in late April to June, but it's the foliage that steals the show. Said to have been discovered by E. A. Bowles in the North Broads, an expanse of wet meadow near Cambridge, England, it was first named 'Aurea' and is still known by that cultivar name in England.

In wet soils, this water-loving sedge may spread into an enormous clump that reaches more than 4 ft. wide. Plant several clumps for a spectacular show and spotlight the effect with green-leaved bog plants.

How to Grow

Full sun to part sun. Wet to very moist soil. Thrives in shallow standing water, but will grow in average garden soil, although with less vigor. Plant divisions in spring. Water deeply in times of drought. Propagate by division.

■ *nigra* p. 127
Black-flowering sedge
Zones 4–8. P/Cl
Height: 6–9 in. Spread: 6 in.

These soft, low clumps of narrow gray-green foliage make a good ground cover, but they spread slowly. Like many sedges, they retain some green leaves throughout the year. New foliage emerges in spring from the old leaves, which recede into a mulch among the plants. Thrives in very moist soil and is good along the edge of a garden pond or pool. The unusual flowers are thick black spikes atop bare stems, held just above the foliage.

California black-flowering sedge *(Carex nudata)* is a similar species with taller, even showier flowers, but it mellows to tawny gold and orange in winter. In the West, this sedge is abundant in lush, moist meadows, where it grows with masses of red and yellow monkey flowers, snapdragon-like plants that adapt easily to life in a garden.

Both sedges offer contrast to pastel-colored astilbes and other perennials. Try them in combination with glossy-leaved bergenias or the tall spears of golden *Iris pseudacorus,* or play up their gray-green leaves with other silvery plants, such as 'Herman's Pride' lamiastrum.

How to Grow

Light shade (*C. nutans* also thrives in full sun). Very moist to boggy soil, even shallow water. Plant divisions in spring. You can let the old foliage die back, or you can cut it back in early spring for a neater look. Propagate by division; plants may also self-sow.

■ *petriei* p. 127
Dwarf brown sedge
Zones 7–9. P/Cl
Height: 4–6 in. Spread: 6 in.

This diminutive grasslike plant is another curiosity of the sedge family, with warm brown foliage year-round. Once you accept the idea that a living plant can be brown, you'll be charmed by this one. Its tendrils of very thin leaves grow in an upright, arching tuft. The flowers never reach above the foliage and add a curly effect when they mature. It's a pretty contrast to taller blue-gray grasses, such as blue Magellan grass *(Agropyron magellanicum)*, which thrives in the moist, well-drained conditions that the sedge requires.

How to Grow
Full sun to shade. Moist but well-drained soil. Work lots of organic matter such as compost, leaf mold, or aged manure into the soil so that it stays moist and fluffy but doesn't get waterlogged. Plant seeds in pots, then transplant to garden, or plant divisions in spring. Water generously during dry times.

■ *plantaginea* *p. 128*
Plantain-leaved sedge
Zones 4–9. P/Cl
Height: 12–24 in. Spread: 8–12 in.
Shade gardeners can enjoy this easy-to-grow sedge as an alternative or a companion to the usual hostas and other shade ground covers. Its flat leaves can reach an inch wide and look something like the common narrow-leaved plantain weed, except that they grow in a clump instead of flat to the ground. The typical spiky sedge flowers are blackish brown and appear in early spring, held well above fresh green leaves. The foliage stays green into winter and needs no cutting back.

The bright green, grassy foliage is an appealing accent in the shade garden. Use it to liven up a bed of deep green periwinkle or to make a hosta planting look new again with a good contrast of color and texture. Also beautiful with ferns, Solomon's-seal, Jacob's-ladder, celandine poppy, and other shade-loving plants.

How to Grow
Light to heavy shade. Moist to average garden soil. Plant divisions in spring. Mulch thickly with chopped dead leaves. Water generously during hot, dry summers. If leaf tips brown excessively during drought or hot weather, trim them off with scissors. Seeds itself when conditions are similar to those of its native Eastern deciduous woodlands.

■ *siderosticha* 'Variegata' *p. 128*
Creeping variegated broad-leaved sedge
Zones 5 or 6–9. P/R
Height: 12–24 in. Spread: 12 in. or more
A striking foliage plant, this sedge sports broad grassy leaves with bold white edges that light up a shady garden. The foliage grows in a continuous sweeping colony rather than in clumps, spreading by underground stolons, but it is easy to keep in control by hand pulling. You can use it as a

spot accent, or let it spread into a ground cover. Try it along a pathway, where the delicate coloring can be admired up close, or use it to highlight a background area of the garden. New shoots are pink when they emerge. Foliage turns golden tan in winter.

How to Grow

Light to medium shade. Moist, rich soil. Plant divisions in spring. Water frequently during dry summers. Cut back in winter or early spring. Propagate by division.

■ *texensis*

Catlin sedge, Texas sedge
Zones 7–10. P/R
Height: 3–4 in. Spread: 6 in.

A native of Texas, this evergreen sedge may be the low-maintenance lawn grass of the future. It's tough and adaptable, staying green even under heavy foot traffic. If you don't mind a slightly looser look than typical lawn grass, Catlin sedge can be just the ticket for creating a greensward. Because it doesn't need mowing, it's also perfect between stepping-stones or as a background for flowering bulbs. Try it as an overplanting for tomasina crocuses, dwarf daffodils, Greek anemones, and other small bulbs, or for the taller varieties of daffodils. The sedge flowers appear in early spring, but they're inconspicuously held against the leaves.

How to Grow

Sun to medium shade. Adaptable to most soils, from very moist to drier-than-average garden soil, and will even grow in shallow standing water. Plant in light or part shade in areas with very hot, dry summers, such as the Southwest. Plant divisions in spring, or for large areas, look for plugs of Catlin sedge, available from lawn-grass suppliers. You can also start seeds in pots, sowing thickly. The sedge needs no cutting back, though you can mow occasionally for a neater look in a lawn. Propagate by division or by seed; the plants self-sow if allowed to set seed, and they have naturalized outside Los Angeles and in some other areas of California.

Chasmanthium

Kaz-man´thee-um
Gramineae. Grass family

Perennial grasses that form clumps or small patches, with uniquely flat seed heads that dangle over the broad leaf blades. Only five species native to eastern North America.

■ *latifolium* *p. 129*
Northern sea oats, spangle grass, wild oats
Zone 4. P/Cl/W
Height: 3–5 ft. Spread: 2 ft. or more

Easy to grow and shade-tolerant, this clump-forming grass makes an excellent ground cover on slopes or open woodland; smaller clumps can accent a pathway or add contrast to a perennial border. The close-set leaves are broad for a grass, green in summer and fall and warm tan in winter. The flat, drooping clusters of oatlike seed heads sway above the leaves in the slightest breeze and look wonderful in winter when displayed against a fence or snow. They last in dried arrangements for more than a year. Spreads fast (by seed) in wet sites, less invasive in dry conditions.

How to Grow
Sun or shade. Looks best in full sun and moist, fertile soil. Tolerates poor or dry soil and heat. Sow seed or increase by division in spring; space 2 ft. apart for mass plantings. Cut back to the ground in early spring.

Coix

ko´icks
Gramineae. Grass family

Tall, branching annual and perennial grasses with flat leaves and abundant flowers springing from the leaf axils. The large, round seeds of some species are used for food and ornament in Southeast Asia. About four species, all of them native to Asia.

■ *lachryma-jobi* *p. 129*
Job's tears
Zones 9–10. PGA/W
Height: 3–6 ft. or more. Spread: 12 in.

This old-fashioned curiosity has been grown for centuries in western gardens and even longer in its native Southeast Asia. Perennial in very mild climates, it can easily be grown as an annual from seed in cold-winter areas. The plant is tall and floppy. With a jointed stem and $1\frac{1}{2}$-in.-wide, 2-ft.-long leaves, it looks almost like corn, and like corn it is neither running nor clump-forming. It usually reaches about 3 ft. tall in the garden but can stretch to 6 ft. Many gardeners consign it to the cutting garden because the seeds are valued more than the ungainly form.

The unusual seeds are shaped like big droplets of tears, which gives the plant its botanical and common names (*lachryma-jobi* translates directly as Job's tears). The nutritious seeds are ground for sweet-tasting meal in some parts of the world. They're also popular for beaded necklaces and clothing decorations, and they've been grown at monasteries since the 14th century for use in rosaries. As the seeds ripen, they turn hard as wood and become beautifully colored — shining white or marked with black, soft gray, or violet, all on the same plant. They ripen at various rates, and the drooping flower clusters may still be blooming or fading when other seeds are mature. They fall off the plant when thoroughly ripe.

How to Grow
Full sun. Fertile, moist but well-drained soil. Easy to grow from seed, but start indoors in pots about eight weeks before the final spring frost date. Transplant to garden after soil has warmed, about corn-planting time.

Cortaderia
Kor-ta-dee´ree-a
Gramineae. Grass family

Perennial grasses that form huge clumps of slender, arching, sharp-edged leaves. Feathery plumes on woody stalks rise in the center of the clumps. About 24 species, native to South America and New Zealand.

■ *selloana* *p. 130*
Pampas grass
Zone 7. P/Cl/W
Height: 8 ft. or more. Spread: 8 ft. or more

Tough as nails but very showy, this grass makes a huge billowing clump of slender leaves that rise up through the center and arch over to the ground; foliage is nearly evergreen in Zone 9, turning tan in colder zones. Cotton candy–like flowering plumes on stiff stalks lift 2 ft. or more above the foliage in late summer and remain showy through midwinter. Female plants are showier than the males. It is most often used as a single specimen in mid-lawn but is perhaps better as a barrier hedge or wind screen, because it gets quite big and the leaf edges are dangerously sharp. 'Rosea' and 'Rubra' have pink plumes. 'Pumila' is a dwarf with flower stalks only 6 ft. tall.

The taller species, *C. jubata,* or purple pampas grass, has become an unwelcome invader in California and other mild areas. (Marin County, California, has banned the sale of seed, considering the plant a noxious weed.) Although still widely offered by nurseries and mail-order catalogs, it's best to avoid planting it and increasing its already strong roothold in America's wildlands. Unfortunately, the difficulties of sorting out pampas grasses, which are variable when grown from seed, means that less-careful nurseries still offer this species under the name "pampas grass," which more correctly belongs to its better-behaved relative, *Cortaderia selloana.* If self-sowing is a problem in your area, it's best to avoid these grasses altogether and plant the noninvasive native *Muhlenbergia rigens* instead.

How to Grow
Full or part sun. Grows anywhere; not fussy about soil or watering. Space 10 ft. apart for mass plantings. Remove old plumes in spring. Cut back old foliage every few years in early spring. Use a gas-powered trimmer with a metal blade; burning it off is an easier solution if allowed in your area. Wear gloves and be careful when working around the sharp-edged leaves. Propagate by division.

■ *selloana* **'Andes Silver'**
'Andes Silver' pampas grass
Zones 6–10. P/Cl/W
Height: 5–7 ft. Spread: 5 ft. or more
More cold-hardy than many cultivars, this stunning pampas grass has billowing plumes of silky, silvery white. Few perennial flowers can hold their own against such magnificence. Luckily, the orange and red blaze of fall foliage begins just in time to match the blooming season of these splendid grasses. The mass of grass leaves and flowers also looks great with brightly colored winter-interest shrubs, including red-twig and yellow-twig dogwoods and red-barked willows.

How to Grow
Same as *Cortaderia selloana*.

■ *selloana* 'Pumila'   *p. 130*
Dwarf pampas grass
Zones 8–10. P/Cl/W
Height: 4–6 ft. Spread: 3 ft.

A plant 3–5 ft. tall isn't usually called a dwarf, unless you're talking about the giants of the pampas grass family. The clumping, arching foliage of this cultivar usually reaches about 3 ft. tall, with the showy plumes carried about 2 ft. above the leaves. Although the plant is smaller than other pampas grasses, the plumes are close to full size. The cultivar blooms in late summer with so many fluffy, erect plumes that it appears a solid mass of golden floss. Dwarf pampas grass often pushes up a few plumes of flowers the first season after planting. It's a gorgeous partner to Japanese maples and right in scale with dwarf mugo pines. Although some catalogs suggest the plant is cold-hardy to Zone 7, it may freeze in cold winters.

How to Grow
Same as *Cortaderia selloana*.

■ *selloana* 'Silver Comet'   *p. 131*
'Silver Comet' pampas grass
Zones 7–10. P/Cl/W
Height: 6–8 ft. Spread: 6 ft.

This tall cultivar has variegated leaves striped with white, a showy effect even before the plant is in bloom. The platinum plumes are gorgeous with the orange foliage of mountain ash, the scarlet of shining sumac, and the deep black-green of spruces. Like other pampas grasses, it benefits from a dark backdrop that offsets the spectacular flowers. Evergreens, such as spruces, firs, and hemlocks, and purple-leaved shrubs such as 'Royal Velvet' smokebush, work magic with pampas grass.

How to Grow
Same as *Cortaderia selloana*.

Cymbopogon
sim-bo-po´gun
Gramineae. Grass family

Perennial, mostly clumping grasses of the tropics, most of them with highly aromatic foliage that yields an oil widely used in cooking, perfumes, and herbal medicines. Includes the plant called nardus *(Cymbopogon nardus)*, the source of citronella oil, which is used as an insect repellent. The genus includes about 30 species, native to India, Ceylon, and other tropical regions of the Old World.

■ *citratus*   *p. 131*
Lemongrass
Zones 9–10. P/Cl/W
Height: 2–6 ft. Spread: 12–24 in. or more

Cooks and tea drinkers know this plant better than gardeners, thanks to its wonderful lemon fragrance and flavor, which is used in herb teas and cooking, especially in Southeast Asian recipes. The plant is also attractive, and its fresh lemon scent is as delightful in the garden as it is in the kitchen. Lemongrass will survive the winter only in warm climates, but it makes a beautiful single-season plant in any area. It grows fast into a clump usually about 3–4 ft. tall and rarely flowers outside of its native home. The foliage springs from bulbous-looking stems, which are often colored a pretty reddish purple. New growth also may have this purplish hue. The 1–1½-in.-wide leaves are soft to the touch.

Plant lemongrass along a walkway where you can pick a bit of leaf as you walk by. Rubbing the leaf between your fingers releases the delicious scent. It thrives in containers, a good choice for cold-winter areas because you can easily move the plant indoors when frost threatens. If your lemongrass does get killed by cold, cut off the foliage with scissors and twist it into a fragrant decoration for the kitchen. To make tea, snip a tablespoon of fresh leaves and steep in hot water for 5 minutes; add honey to taste.

How to Grow
Full sun to part shade. Average garden soil. Grows well in a pot, but it's a thirsty plant and needs frequent watering; if the soil dries out completely and the foliage dies, cut it back for new growth. If you grow it in the garden in cold-winter areas, slice off a division in late summer and pot it up to bring indoors in fall. Several weeks in a container outside will allow the new plant to get established in its pot. Keep on a sunny windowsill and replant in the garden after the soil is warm in midspring. Propagate by division.

Cyperus

sy´per-us

Cyperaceae. Sedge family

Annual and perennial plants usually with bare stems topped by an arching cluster of leaflike bracts that open like an umbrella, giving the genus its common name, umbrella sedge. Some sprout true leaves from the base of the plant. Generally, annual umbrella sedges have fibrous roots; perennials grow from rhizomes, which spread, but not fast enough to be called "running."

Most of the 600 or so species are tropical and subtropical natives, from South Africa and Madagascar among other homelands, but some, including the pesky lawn weed called yellow nut sedge *(C. esculentus)*, are naturalized in North America. The unusual form of the plant is eye-catching in the garden. Tender species also make good container plants, especially in and around water gardens, and can be lifted and stored in a protected place in cold-winter areas. Some umbrella sedges are grown as houseplants.

■ *albostriatus*

(C. diffusus; C. diffusus 'Elegans'; *C. elegans)*

Broad-leaved umbrella plant

Zones 9–10. P

Height: 6–24 in., but usually 18–20 in. Spread: 18–24 in.

A beautiful perennial that adds tropical grace to a shaded garden with moist soil. Soft, leafy bracts, to ¾ in. wide and 6 in. long, form a broad umbrella atop the stems. Delicate umbels of fine tan spikelets rise from the center of the canopy like a small, airy bouquet. True leaves at the base of the clump may grow as tall as the flowering stems. The plant spreads slowly from a woody rhizome.

Originally from South Africa, this sedge grows best in damp, shady places, which makes it a perfect companion for hostas and ferns. It's also striking with orange-red impatiens in a pot or in the garden. Like other umbrella sedges, it looks great along the water. 'Variegatus' is an appealing variegated cultivar with understated cream to yellow or lime-green striping along the leaves.

How to Grow

Part to moderate shade; moist to wet soil. Thrives in fertile soils, but also grows in average soil. Does well in humid climates. Dig and divide the rhizomes to propagate. Foliage is interesting in arrangements as well as in the garden. Grow the plant in pots in the water garden, but don't totally submerge the roots.

■ *alternifolius* *p. 132*
Umbrella plant
Zones 9–10. P
Height: 18–36 in. Spread: 18–36 in.

This adaptable perennial sedge grows in a dense clump of tall bare stems crowned by drooping umbrellas of leaflike bracts. Dark green like the stems, the bracts are usually about a half-inch wide or less and reach as long as 10–12 in., giving them an elegant, spidery look. The smooth, leggy stems remain uncluttered by true leaves at the base, and sprays of small flowers top the bracts. The plant expands slowly from rhizomes.

Originating in the marshes of Madagascar, Mauritius, and other islands, umbrella plant is found throughout the tropics and subtropics. It's a natural in a garden setting near water or with bog plants, but it can also be a centerpiece in a moist-soil garden or in a container, and it makes an interesting houseplant.

How to Grow

Sun to part shade. Must have at least moist soil; thrives in shallow water and in wet soils. Excellent pond plant submerged in a tub. Grows best in fertile soil. Sun and wind in hot climates will burn the foliage, making it turn brown. The bracts will turn brown if nipped by temperatures lower than 32°F; the root will die in cold below about 15°F. Snip off brown tips to neaten its appearance. In a serious case of sun- or windburn, or if the plant is touched by frost, cut the damaged stems to the ground, give the plant a dose of liquid fertilizer, water well if not growing in wet soil, and watch it push up new stalks. In cold climates, winter the plant indoors in a well-lit area. Set the pot in a tray of water or on wet gravel, and mist frequently to boost humidity. Easiest propagation is by division, but you can also grow from seed or try floating the inflorescences upside down on water; they may sprout new shoots.

■ *papyrus p. 132*
Papyrus, Egyptian papyrus, Egyptian paper reed
Zones 9–10. P
Height: 6–15 ft. Spread: 3 ft. or more
The first paper was made by pressing the pithy stems of this plant into a corrugated surface suitable for decorating. Some suggest papyrus is also the "bulrush" with which Moses' cradle was disguised. Aside from these useful possibilities, papyrus is an artistic accent in any garden. Its thin, threadlike bracts, up to 18 in. long, create a profusion of shimmering, arching sprays atop bare stems an inch or two wide. The small flowers turn into brown nutlike fruits that dot the center of each spray. This is a big plant but an airy one. It makes an elegant showpiece for the water garden or the patio. Combine with water lilies, lotus, and other plants with big, simple leaves for contrast.

'Mexico' is a slightly different cultivar introduced to the California garden trade. It has denser heads than the species, thanks to an interesting trait of the bracts: each emerges singly from the umbel, then splits into two threads about 8–12 in. from the center, giving the plant heads an exceptionally lush look. An individual cluster can be 18–24 in. in diameter.

How to Grow
Full sun or part shade. In soil that is constantly very moist, or in water up to 3 ft. deep. Grow potted in pool and ponds or plant in earth-bottom water gardens; settle a potted plant on supporting bricks or stones in the bottom of a large, water-filled container for patio use; add a few minnows from a bait shop to keep down mosquito larvae. Clip off any past-their-prime seed heads or broken stems. To propagate, divide the knotted rhizomes (try a sharp spade or hatchet), or grow from seed. Floating inflorescences may sprout new shoots. The beauty of this plant is worth the trouble of overwintering in cold areas, but its size makes a greenhouse or sunroom almost a must.

■ *profiler p.133*
(*C. isocladus; C. papyrus* 'Nanus')
Dwarf papyrus
Zones 9–10. P
Height: 12–36 in. Spread: 12 in. or more

Like an impertinent young cousin, this umbrella plant has a livelier, less refined attitude than other members of the family. Instead of drooping gracefully, its bracts stick up like a hedgehog's bristles. The brushy umbels of bracts are glossy, light to medium green, and usually about 3–4 in. across. At 2–3 ft. high, the plant is a miniature when compared to the 15-ft. true papyrus. It's a good scale for a small pool or aquarium. Try dwarf papyrus with red-leaved cannas along the water; its texture and color will liven up the staid, broad leaves of the cannas.

How to Grow
Part shade or light shade. Wet, fertile soil or in water. Prevent drying out; without water, plants may go into a sharp and often irreversible decline. Good container plant, but insert the plastic planting pot into another container filled with water. As umbels go to seed and brown, clip them off to keep the plant looking fresh and green. Easiest propagation is by dividing the creeping rhizomes. You can also grow from seed or float the inflorescences upside down on water to try sprouting new shoots.

Dasylirion
Das-i-leer´ee-on
Agavaceae. Agave family
Woody-based perennials with very short or sometimes medium-height trunks topped with dense clusters of long, slender, often spiny-edged leaves. The rounded leaf base is called a desert spoon. About 18 species native to the Southwest and Mexico.

■ *texanum* p. 133
Sotol, bear grass
Zones 8–10. P/Cl
Height: 2–3 ft. Spread: 3 ft. or more
A rounded mound of spiky leaves 2–3 ft. long and $1/2$–1 in. wide radiates from the stubby trunk of this perennial like a giant pincushion. The short trunk may be totally underground, so that the plant looks like a clump of grass from a distance. Older plants spread underground to form a clump of rosettes. Leaves are medium to dark green with yellowish spines along the margin. Slender flower stalks up to 15 ft. tall and topped with wormlike clusters of small greenish, yellow, or white flowers arise in late spring and last for several weeks.
The leaves of the plant have been used for thousands of years as thatch and in basketry by native people of the desert

Southwest and Mexico, and the leaf fibers have been turned into string and rope. An alcoholic drink called *sotol* is also made from the plant. Useful for desert gardens, combined with succulents and shrubs, and interesting in a container (but keep away from passersby; the leaves are sharp). Several other species are offered by native plant nurseries.

How to Grow
Full to part sun. Needs good drainage. Thrives in hot, dry sites, unamended soil, and caliche. Remove old bloom stalks. Needs no other maintenance.

Deschampsia

Des-champs´ee-uh
Gramineae. Grass family
   Clumping, mostly perennial grasses with rough leaves and masses of delicate-looking flower stalks. About 50 species, most native to cool regions in the Northern Hemisphere.

■ *caespitosa* *p. 134*
Tufted hair grass
Zones 4–9. P/Cl/C
Height: 2–3 ft. Spread: 2 ft.
   A North American native and once the dominant grass in mountain meadows, this cool-season grass was valued for forage because it greened up early. The species and several varieties also occur in the ever-shrinking bogs and wet places from Greenland to North Carolina, west to Illinois and in some western states, and in arctic and temperate areas of the Old World. The plant was first valued for garden use in Europe, so unless you find a supplier that uses regional plants as stock, your tufted hair grass is likely to be of Eurasian extraction.
   Excellent for mass plantings, tufted hair grass creates a delicate cloud of bloom from late spring through summer. The flowers are held in panicles that can reach 5 ft. tall above mounds of spiky or arching foliage. They are pale greenish yellow tinged with purple and ripen to golden tan. Plant the grass against a dark background to show off the flowers to best effect, or use it in a woodland garden where the glistening panicles add light and airiness. Foliage is evergreen or semievergreen even in northern climates (it has remained green at temperatures lower than –13°F), so you can also include this species in a border of plants for winter interest. Cut flowers can be used in fresh or dried bouquets. 'Tardiflora' blooms two to three weeks later than the species. 'Bronze

Veil' ('Bronzeschleier') produces a golden brown cloud of drooping panicles that almost hides the foliage. (See photo on p. 134.) 'Gold Pendant' ('Goldgehange') has rich golden yellow clouds of flowers. A single plant is strong enough to command attention in the garden, or you can group them for extra effect. (See photo on p. 135.) Try 'Gold Pendant' along water or in a woodland garden with witch hazel, corylopsis, and other shrubs. Also beautiful with purple-leaved smoke tree, even when the flowers are past their prime. Tufted hair grass also makes a good turf grass in low-traffic areas. In Pebble Beach, California, it is planted on golf course roughs, where it goes dormant in late summer but remains attractive as a low, golden, undulating surface.

How to Grow
Part shade or moderate shade. Will grow in sun, but growth and bloom will not be as good as in shade. Tolerates acidic or alkaline conditions if the soil is fertile and moist. Plant 2 ft. apart in masses for best effect. Cut flower stalks back in late summer, or let the fine bleached stems stand through the winter. Cut foliage to the crown in early spring (or early summer where summers are hot). Cold-hardy but doesn't take heat well. A long-lived, unfussy plant. May self-sow. Propagate by division or seed. In coastal central California, bales of this grass are now widely available. The grass is harvested as hay when seeds are mature; to plant, simply spread the hay on the selected area.

■ *caespitosa* 'Holciformis'
(D. holciformis)
Pacific hair grass
Zones 8–9. P/Cl/C
Height: 18–24 in. Spread: 18–24 in.

This cultivar has the same erect, tufted foliage as the species in a lighter shade of green, but its flowers are very different. Instead of being carried in light, open, branching panicles, they're narrow, slightly arching wands thick with flowers and then seeds. They mature to a beautiful golden yellow. The grass blooms early and the foliage stays evergreen. Other cultivars and the species flag in hot, sunny climates; this one does not.

Once a common native in marshes, sandy soil, and coastal prairies from Vancouver Island to central California and along the Big Sur coast, 'Holciformis' has a wilder look than the species. It is best used in naturalistic plantings, where its bleached panicles will reflect the natural cycle of seasons like the wild grasses of the mountain foothills.

How to Grow

Sun or part shade. Does best in moist soil but will also tolerate dry, even sandy, soil. Cut back after flowering for neatness.

■ *flexuosa*
(Aira flexuosa)
Crinkled hair grass, wavy hair grass
Zones 4–8. P/Cl/C
Height: 8–12 in. Spread: 8–12 in.

A delicate-looking but tough little treasure with a tuft of slender leaves and a bouquet of slim-stemmed flower spikelets. Purplish or bronze when they emerge in summer, the inflorescences mellow to a fine gold that makes a shimmering haze when backlit by the sun.

Native to dry or rocky woods, slopes, and open ground in the Northern Hemisphere, it lends a dainty presence to woodland gardens and shady borders. It's also beautiful at the top of a slope, where afternoon light can highlight its branching panicles. Mingle patches of crinkled hair grass with heathers and heaths, or try it in a planting of shiny-leaved bearberry *(Arctostaphlyos uva-ursi)*. In arrangements, fresh or dried, it's as airy as baby's-breath.

How to Grow

Grows best in acidic soil high in humus or other organic matter. Does well in moist soil but also thrives in dry shade; tolerates drought. Part shade or light to moderate shade; sun in cool northern climates. Divide to propagate, or start from seed. (Cultivars, except for the golden-leaved 'Aurea', probably will not come true from seed.) May self-sow, cropping up in unexpected niches, especially among rocks.

Elymus

el′ih-mus
Gramineae. Grass family

The wild rye grasses are mostly perennials, tufted or rhizomatous; some are so vigorously invasive that they are planted for dune control. About 50 species are included in the genus, all native to the temperate Northern Hemisphere, from Russia and Eurasia to Canada, Alaska, and California. Leaves are stiff and may be dangerously sharp, especially the tips.

■ *arenarius* 'Glaucus' *p. 135*
(*Leymus arenarius* 'Glaucus')
Blue Lyme grass, blue wild rye, blue European beach grass
Zones 4–10. P/R/W
Height: 1–2 ft. Spread: 2 ft. or more

The gray-blue foliage of this loose, open grass is so tempting to include in the perennial border that many gardeners move it right in despite its well-deserved reputation for aggressiveness. The unearthly blue color combines well with almost any perennial, especially those with pink, white, or red flowers. The spiky-looking leaves are surprisingly soft to the touch; the edges, however, are sharp enough to slice an unwary finger. Flowers look like narrow heads of grain.

The native *Elymus glaucus,* or blue wild rye, is a striking blue-green. The noninvasive plant grows quickly into a tight bunch with large broad leaves and stems that reach 2–3 ft. tall. The clump eventually reaches the size of a bushel basket at the base. It thrives in part shade and does best in moist soil. Grow from seed.

How to Grow
Highly adaptable. Plant in sun to part or light shade, in any soil. Thrives in dry conditions. It has a tendency to become floppy and somewhat open; keep it compact and in good color by occasionally cutting it back to the crown. Propagate by division. Unless you're growing the grass for erosion control, contain its spread with sunken barriers or by planting in a bucket.

■ *condensatus* 'Canyon Prince' *p. 136*
(*Leymus condensatus* 'Canyon Prince')
'Canyon Prince' wild rye, giant wild rye
Zones 7–9. P/Cl/C
Height: 18–24 in. Spread: 18–24 in.

Another superb silvery blue grass, this selection forms a mound of stiff upright leaves. It spreads much more slowly than *E. arenarius* 'Glaucus', so it's a better choice for the perennial border. Also outstanding in foliage gardens or with shrubs. The narrow spikes of flowers rise to 6 ft. above the foliage.

How to Grow
A recent introduction, found growing wild along the California coast, this grass's adaptability is still being tested. Thrives in full sun and in shade, and apparently in most soils, including heavy clay and sand. Does well beneath oaks. Cut back when foliage loses its blue color. Propagate by division.

■ *tritichoides*   *p. 136*
(Leymus tritichoides)
Creeping wild rye, beardless wild rye
Zones 7–10. P/R/W
Height: 2–4 ft. Spread: 2 ft. or more

A fast-spreading native grass of the American West, this green to blue-green species colonizes large areas with its spreading, scaly rhizomatous roots. Inflorescences look like slim heads of grain without the "beard" hairs. Native to moist soils from Montana to Baja California and Washington State, it hybridizes with other wild species; varieties that differ in size, foliage color, and habit are also common. Good for masses or ground cover; keep it out of the mixed border. Excellent for controlling erosion on slopes.

How to Grow
Sun to part or light shade. Moist to dry soils. Seems as adaptable and as tenacious as other species in this genus. Becomes dormant during periods of drought; cut back and water to encourage new growth. Propagate by division.

Equisetum

eh-kwih-see´tum
Equisetaceae. Horsetail family

The 35 or so species of horsetails are primitive plants that have remained unchanged since the days of the dinosaurs. They have noticeably jointed stems, and some species have whorls of leaves or branches at the joints (which gives the genus its common name, horsetail). The leafless species look like grass from a distance, especially when they spread to carpet a stream bank or hillside. Related to ferns, they reproduce by spores, which are formed in small pine cone–like structures at the tops of the stems.

The bare-stemmed species are popular in California landscaping and around water gardens, although they're adaptable enough to grow almost anywhere. Horsetails are found just about everywhere in the world except Australia and New Zealand.

■ *hyemale*   *p. 137*
Scouring rush
Zones 5–10. P/R
Height: 18–48 in. Spread: 18 in. or more

A vigorous, erect perennial with cylindrical stems that sprout thickly from creeping rhizomes. At a distance the rush looks like a swath of tall green grass, but up close you can see the plant's interesting jointed stems. The $1/4$–$3/8$-in.-thick stems are marked at the closely spaced joints with off-white bands and black fringes. The stems are loaded with grains of silica, the rough substance that gives the plant its common name, scouring rush. Native Americans used it to scrub cooking vessels and showed European settlers how to do the same. Some used the plant fresh; others burned masses of it and used the high-silica wood ashes as a scrubbing powder. If you grow this interesting plant, you can give it a try yourself — a bundled-up handful of stems works better than a plastic pad on glass casserole dishes or the outdoor grill (but keep it away from Teflon).

In its native haunts, scouring rush usually grows in wet places or along water and in the East can often be found growing near winterberry holly *(Ilex verticillata)*. Excellent beside pools and in bog gardens; it is also a common landscape accent and planter subject in southern California. The simple upright form looks great in a large clay or decorated pot and its spare lines are used to complement modern architecture. The matte dark green stems keep their color all year, which makes this a good plant to grow in mass for winter interest. Add a clump of tawny miscanthus for a lovely vignette in the snow.

How to Grow
Sun to shade. Almost any soil, from waterlogged clay to dry, sandy soil. Plants are shorter and slower to spread in dry soils. Colonizes by creeping rhizomes; keep it in place with barriers of plastic buried 10 in. or deeper and pull up any errant roots. Cut back dead brown or gray stems as needed or let them fall naturally. The silica-loaded stems will dull your pruning shears in just one session, as if you'd been cutting through sandpaper. Propagate by division.

■ *scirpoides* var. *contorta*
Contorted dwarf scouring rush, miniature contorted horsetail
Zones 6–10. P/R
Height: 2–6 in. Spread: 6 in. or more
This unusual little horsetail has stems as thin as fine wire and as gently curved as a head of wavy hair. The texture makes you want to reach out and pat the plant. The stems are dotted with the typical light bands at the joints. The niceties of this miniature are best appreciated at close range, so try it in a pretty container on a patio table, or spotlight it between stones along the edge of a pool.

How to Grow

Sun to light shade. Moist to wet soil of average to rich fertility. Will also thrive in shallow water. Don't let this one dry out; it has a hard time recovering from a dry spell. Rhizomes creep slowly to expand the plant but are easy to control if needed. Slice off pieces with a sharp trowel to propagate.

Eragrostis

air-uh-grahss´tis

Gramineae. Grass family

The beauty of many of the species in this large genus is reason enough for the name love grass, a direct translation of the botanical name, *Eros* for love and *agrostis,* a grass. The genus includes some 250 annual and perennial grasses, widely distributed in North and South America as well as Eurasia, Australia, and Africa. Habit varies from mounding perennials to lax, crabgrasslike annuals. Some love grasses provide valuable forage in difficult conditions; the rigid stems of *E. obtusiflora,* for instance, have gotten many an animal through hard times in the dusty, alkali soils of the West.

■ *curvula* *p. 137*

Weeping love grass

Zones 7–10. P/Cl/W

Height: 12–24 in. Spread: 18–24 in

This mounding grass is a common sight along roadways in Arizona, Texas, Florida, and other mild-winter states, but it actually comes from the mountains of Tanganyika. Introduced in the 1920s to the South and Southwest by the U.S. Department of Agriculture to control erosion and revegetate grasslands, it slipped the bounds and is now part of the naturalized flora. Not nearly as pushy as other U.S.D.A. mistakes, weeping love grass is beautiful, with fine, flowing texture like a mane of hair in a shampoo commercial. The dark green foliage turns reddish tan, then straw-colored in winter; it stays evergreen in climates without frost. Arching, open panicles of delicate flowers rise above the clump in fall; look closely and you can see the wavy undulations of the panicle branches that give the plant its botanical name. Plant on slopes, where you can appreciate the flowing form of the foliage, in the perennial border or a mixed-grass planting. Its relaxed attitude also looks good along a wood fence or stone wall.

How to Grow

Sun. Grows well in almost all soils as long as they are well drained. Thrives in sandy soils; exceptionally drought-tolerant. Cut back old foliage in early spring. Self-sows in mild climates. Start from seed sown in pots or propagate by division.

■ *spectabilis*
Purple love grass
Zones 5–9. P/Cl/W
Height: 12–18 in. Spread: 6–18 in.

In late summer and early fall, a cloud of soft reddish purple covers the plant like a haze of smoke along the ground. It's hard to believe that a single small tuft produces enough hazy bloom to span a 3–4-ft. area. The gauzy effect is created by fine-stemmed, many-branched panicles of delicate flowers. After the seed heads mature and drop, the spent flower heads often break off and roll along the ground like tumbleweeds. This grass is beautiful in the border or in masses. Try it with dwarf pink or white zinnias and tall grasses, or with late-blooming perennials, such as sedum 'Autumn Joy', blue mistflower *(Eupatorium coelestinum)*, purple coneflowers, or New England asters.

How to Grow

Sun. Average to light soils; must be well drained. Excellent in sandy soil. Also grows well in clay, as long as it doesn't stay waterlogged. Give it space; don't overcrowd. Usually doesn't need cutting back — old foliage dies back in spring as new growth pushes out — but you can neaten it up if needed. Start from seed; it may self-sow. Propagate well-established plants by division.

■ *trichodes* 'Bend'
'Bend' sand love grass
Zones 5–9. P/Cl/W
Height: 2–5 ft. Spread: 1–2 ft.

The glossy leaves of this fine-textured but substantial grass rise in tufts, then bend sharply at the top. In summer, fine-branched, arching panicles emerge in a cloud of shimmering pinkish bronze. The flower heads are so profuse they may spill over, eventually making the plant weep and sometimes collapse. A circular wire support set halfway up the foliage before bloom will help the grass hold its head up. Plant as a single specimen in a mixed perennial border, or in groups. The flowers make a graceful bouquet in a slim vase.

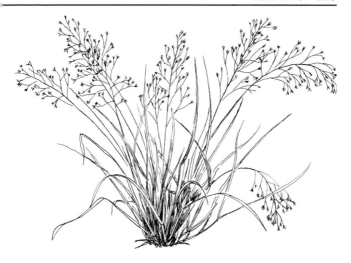

How to Grow

Sun. Average soil. Semievergreen; cut back before new growth begins in early spring. Propagate by division or seed. Self-sows in mild-winter areas.

Erianthus

air-ee-an´thus
Gramineae. Grass family
   Perennial grasses with tall reedy stems, flat spreading leaf blades, and silky flowering plumes. About 20 species, native to temperate and tropical climates. Some botanists now combine *Erianthus* with *Saccharum,* the genus that includes sugar cane.

■ *ravennae* *p. 138*
(Saccharum ravennae)
Ravenna grass, plume grass, hardy pampas grass
Zones 6–10. P/Cl/W
Height: 9–12 ft. Spread: 5–6 ft.
   A dramatic grass for large landscapes, ravenna looks a lot like pampas grass *(Cortaderia selloana).* Its flower plumes, up to 2 ft. long, last from September through winter, lightening from purplish to beige to silver. Cut them to use for fresh or dried arrangements. The pleasantly fuzzy stalks hold plumes well above 1-in.-wide leaves, which are soft on top but like sandpaper underneath. Although big, this plant is not invasive — it forms a clump and doesn't spread. Keep the mature

size in mind when placing it in the garden; beside a patio or next to a narrow walkway it would be overwhelming, but it makes a good screen or backdrop for a border. You'll enjoy its constant movement and rustling sound on breezy days. In mild climates, it may self-sow and spread beyond the garden; it has become naturalized in Arizona.

How to Grow
Full sun. Best in relatively infertile, dry soil, where it stays upright and strong; requires staking in fertile or moist conditions. Cut old stalks to the ground in early spring. Propagate by division or start from seed. May self-sow.

Eriophorum
air-ee-o´for-um
Cyperaceae. Sedge family
    The cotton grasses are neither grasses nor cotton, but they are still well named. All bear the signature tufts of fluffy white flowers from which the genus gets its name (*erion* is Greek for wool). The genus includes about 30 species of annual and perennial grasslike plants, usually evergreen, which may grow in clumps or spread by rhizomes. Floating on cottony fibers, the seeds are quick to colonize damp marshes and bogs. Native to the north temperate zone and the Arctic, cotton grasses are a common sight on the tundra; they languish in warm climates.

■ *latifolium* *p. 138*
Cotton grass
Zones 4–8. P/Cl/W
Height: 8–18 in. Spread: 12 in.
    This charming grasslike perennial bestows a sense of humor on the garden. Its white cotton balls emerge in spring and dance across marshy sites like the tails of a hundred Easter bunnies, making them irresistible to kids and older garden visitors alike. The thin, spiky leaves grow in erect clumps, and the plant forms colonies by self-sowing. Try cotton grass in a naturalized wet meadow or along the edge of a pond.

How to Grow
Sun. Moist or wet acidic soil that mirrors native bog conditions; will also grow in average garden soil if watered frequently. Best in cool climates. Propagate by seed or divide established plants. May self-sow.

Festuca

fess-too´kuh

Gramineae. Grass family

Many popular ornamental grasses and valuable lawn and forage grasses belong to this genus of over 300 perennial species. They occur throughout the world but are most abundant in temperate and cold regions including Eurasia, North Africa, and North America. They are generally clumping plants with some tall and coarse-bladed, such as *Festuca elatior,* or English bluegrass, a commonly grown pasture grass. The ornamental types are usually springy tussocks or mats of fine, wiry foliage, often blue-gray in color; they are beautiful and useful, but unfortunately, mostly short-lived.

A note on nomenclature: Like many other grasses, fescues are often sold under different botanical names for the same plant, and identification is often confused. Alternative names are listed in the descriptions that follow. Many of the ornamental cultivars developed in Germany are listed in catalogs by their German names; some suppliers use English translations. Both are provided in these plant descriptions.

■ *amethystina* *p. 139*

(*F. ovina* 'Glauca')

Sheep's fescue, tufted fescue, large blue fescue

Zones 4–8. P/Cl/C

Height: 8–12 in. Spread: 12 in.

A cool-season evergreen grass that grows in weeping clumps of very fine foliage, usually of a blue-gray cast. Panicles of dainty flowers are deep gray-blue at first and ripen to golden tan and beige. It's at its best in spring, and it languishes in summer humidity.

The plants grow in neat tufted mounds, perfect for edging a bed or pathway. They can also be combined with perennials such as cottage pinks and catmint in a mixed border, or grown close together as a ground cover, though they won't last much beyond three years and will need replacing as they decline. Cultivars offer improvements on the species; try 'Bronzeglanz' ('Bronze Glaze' or 'Bronze Luster') for showy flowers and bronze-hued foliage, or 'Klose', an olive-green fescue with extra-fine texture and blue-colored new growth. 'Superba' has excellent blue-gray color and purple-stemmed flowers that ripen to tan; clip them off if you don't care for their color against the foliage.

How to Grow

Sun; light shade in hot-summer climates. Light, moist but very well drained soil. Cut back after flowering if plant looks shabby. This is a short-lived plant. Propagate by division or by seed.

■ *gautieri* *p. 139*
(*F. scoparia*)
Bearskin fescue
Zones 4–6. P/Cl/C
Height: 4 in. Spread: 4 in.

The dense, bright green clumps of this fescue form neat cushions that invite patting — but beware. The leaves will jab you like a million needle pricks. The deception is no reason to avoid growing it. The tight mounds are ideal for carefully maintained rock gardens or troughs of alpines, where this native of the Pyrenees will feel most at home. It's a charming companion to dwarf columbines. The cultivar 'Pic Carlit' is a more compact variety.

How to Grow
Part to moderate shade. Average to dry soils. Extremely drought-tolerant. Though tough, this little grass demands perfect drainage and does best in cool conditions. Give the plant several inches of bare space around it and lighten the soil with plenty of gravel. Propagate by careful division.

■ *glauca* *(see below for photos)*
(*F. ovina, F. ovina* 'Glauca', *F. ovina* var. *glauca, F. cinerea*)
Blue fescue, blue sheep's fescue, gray fescue
Zones 4–9. P/Cl/C
Height: 8–18 in. Spread: 8–12 in.

The versatility of this grass makes it one of the most popular ornamentals. Fine, wiry leaves form a dense cushion of striking blue-gray that combines well with plants of all colors. The species gets its name from the word "glaucous," referring to a thin gray coating on the leaves that rubs off as easily as the bloom on grapes. Blue fescues are cool-season grasses, which means most of them go dormant in summer heat. Some cultivars hold their color even in hot weather. Most are evergreen (or "everblue") in milder winters.

The list of synonyms above testifies to the confusion of classification of these grasses. The simplest solution for the gardener, if not the botanist, is to ask for the named cultivar (see the list on the facing page), which will give you the best chance of getting the plant you want, regardless of whether it is classed as *Festuca cinerea, F. glauca,* or something else.

Use groups of blue fescue between flowering perennials in the border to intensify pinks and other pastels, to highlight whites, cool down hot reds and oranges, or separate colors that might clash, such as salmon and bubblegum pink. Try them with grasses of contrasting color, such as red-leaved cultivars like 'Warrior' switch grass (*Panicum virgatum* 'Warrior') and flame grass (*Miscanthus sinensis* 'Purpurascens').

They also look great with coarser gray-leaved grasses, including blue oat grass *(Helictotrichon sempervirens)* and 'Heavy Metal' switch grass (*Panicum virgatum* 'Heavy Metal'). When other grasses are cloaked in winter colors of wheat and straw, the cool gray cushions of blue stand out like a mirror reflecting the sky.

Fine texture and regular shape make blue fescues a good choice for edging borders and paths, accompanying small conifers and alpine perennials in rock gardens, and covering small patches of ground. Planted in mounds about 8–10 in. apart, they create a look like a billowy gray sea. They are ill suited, however, for steep hillsides or other sites that are not easily accessible. The plants keep a distinctly mounded form that makes weeding around them necessary, and their short life span (usually three years or less) means that older specimens must be replaced as they expire.

How to Grow

Sun; light to part shade in hot-summer areas. Very well drained, average to fertile soil. Best in areas without high summer humidity. Drought-tolerant. Cut back when plant looks shabby or the mound loses its compactness. An annual early spring haircut, to 3 in. above the crown, will keep plants looking fresh and new. Many go dormant in summer; cut back to crown and they will regrow when cooler weather and moisture return in fall. Keep a fresh supply of plants by taking small divisions from established clumps each spring. If the mound dies out in the center, dig up, slice into sections, and replant.

Propagate by division or seed. Division will ensure the same traits as in the parent. If you're the adventurous type, try growing blue fescues from seed. They won't all look the same — some will be taller, others shorter; some mounded, others more erect; some blue, some green.

As blue fescue has gained in popularity, the number of cultivars on the market has skyrocketed. The following are particularly noteworthy; German names are given in parentheses. All thrive in Zones 4–9 and can be grown as described below. Unless otherwise noted, all grow upwards of 8 in. high and wide.

'Blue Glow' ('Blauglut') is outstanding among fescues for its intense blue-gray foliage. On the small side, it grows to 6 in. high and wide and holds up well to summer heat.

'Blue-Silver' ('Blau Silber') is another excellent silvery blue cultivar that almost glows in the garden. It stays beautiful even in hot summers. One of the best for eastern and midwestern summers. (See p. 140.)

'Elijah's Blue' is one of the palest cultivars, with foliage of a light silver-blue. It makes a striking companion to strong-colored flowers, such as deep purple *Campanula glomerata* or Siberian iris 'Caesar's Brother', or with brilliant red Oriental poppies. (See p. 140.)

'Sea Urchin' ('Seeigel') is a very fine textured, springy clump of green rather than blue-gray foliage. An interesting accent in a perennial border or edging, it also makes a good ground cover. (See p. 141.)

'Solling' doesn't flower and is therefore a good choice for those who like the foliage effect of blue fescue but find the flowers distracting. The beautiful clump of fine leaves feels like soft steel wool to the touch, and the plants knit together into an almost seamless turf if placed closely.

'Tom Thumb' ('Daeumling') makes a dainty tuft about 4 in. high and 4–6 in. wide. New growth is soft blue-gray-green, changing to green with maturity. It's good for an accent in a small-scale garden or for an edging.

■ *muelleri*   *p. 141*
Mueller's fescue
Zones 5–9. P/Cl/C
Height: 6–8 in. Spread: 6–8 in.
   This cool-season perennial grass grows in soft, fine-textured mounds of thin, wiry foliage. It's one of the best green fescues for the garden and occasionally may show a touch of blue-green in certain light. A more erect but coarser green fescue is *F. mairei,* Moroccan fescue.

How to Grow
Like *F. glauca.*

Glyceria
glih-seer´ee-uh
Gramineae. Grass family
   The deliciously sweet seeds of the species *Glyceria fluitans* have given the genus its common names sweet grass and manna grass. These good-tasting forage grasses, including *G. elata,* a native grass of the moist Northwest woods, fowl manna grass *(G. striata),* and others, are like candy to ducks and other waterfowl, who seek them out in moist meadows and other wet places. The 16 perennial species in this genus

hail from Australia, New Zealand, South America, and the northern temperate zone, most of them native to marshes and shallow water.

Many manna grasses are tall and reedlike, but they vary in habit, and their flowers can be narrow spikes or large, open, branched panicles. Most spread by creeping rhizomatous roots. They are excellent plants for wildlife gardeners, but only the species below is commonly sold in the ornamental trade.

■ *maxima (see below for photo)*
Manna grass, reed sweet grass, reed manna grass
Zones 5–10. P/R/W
Height: 2–6 ft., usually 2–3 ft. Spread: 4 ft. or more

This tall, reedlike perennial grass spreads by rhizomatous roots to form large stands. The $\frac{1}{4}$–$\frac{1}{2}$-in.-wide leaves are long and coarse in texture, but the large panicles of flowers have a delicate grace. An aquatic grass that grows well in shallow water or wet soils, it's a good plant for large ponds, where it holds its own along the water's edge with other aggressive plants like cattails (*Typha* spp.) and yellow flag iris (*Iris pseudacorus*). It may be too unruly for small, restrained water gardens.

Variegated manna grass ('Variegata') is a bright-colored cultivar. (See p. 142.) New foliage emerges with a pretty pink tint, then changes to ivory and then to yellow, with green stripes becoming noticeable in summer. The plant has a casually erect-arching habit, with leaves bending over near the tips or at various heights. It's a fast spreader, so give it space where it can grow en masse.

How to Grow
Sun. Moist to wet soil or in water (to 2 ft. deep); also grows in average moist garden soil, where it is less inclined to spread. Think before you plant; this is a fast mover and difficult to get back in bounds. Propagate by division.

Hakonechloa
hah-ko-neh-klo´uh
Gramineae. Grass family

This genus includes only a single species, a graceful, spreading mound of arching foliage most familiar to gardeners in its golden-variegated form. These slow-growing plants are expensive, but if your budget allows, they make a gorgeous ground cover. Hakonechloa grows in the wild on the Japanese island of Honshu, where it finds a roothold on the rocky cliffs and spreads by creeping stolons.

■ *macra* *p. 142*
Hakonechloa, hakone grass
Zones 4–10. P/Cl/W
Height: 12–30 in. Spread: 24 in. or more

This perennial Japanese forest grass is rich green in its natural species form. The loose, spilling foliage is so beautiful that the fine-seeded fall inflorescences are almost an afterthought. It has the quality of an elegant, low-growing bamboo for shade gardens, setting off the wide leaves and formal habit of hostas with its flowing grace. Its smooth leaves turn rusty orange-bronze in autumn, a beautiful effect with fall-blooming witch hazels or with the flaking bark of river birches or parrotia.

How to Grow
Part to moderate shade; shade in hot-summer regions. Moist but well-drained, humusy soil. Water generously when rainfall is scarce. A beautiful plant worth the bit of extra trouble to make it happy. Spreads very slowly by creeping roots. Grows taller in cool climates. Cut back old foliage when needed. Propagate by division.

■ *macra* 'Aureola' *p. 143*
(*H. macra* 'Urahajusa Zuku')
Golden hakonechloa, golden hakone grass
Zones 4–10. P/Cl/W
Height: 12–24 in. Spread: 18 in.

Many gardeners would rate this the most beautiful ornamental grass of all. Its lovely golden leaves spill over from their wiry stems like a waterfall, not just in a single mound but in a series of cascading sprays that give the plant a fluid motion. The buttery yellow leaves are slightly streaked with green. In fall their color intensifies to pink, at first just at the tips and edges, but eventually the whole plant is a rich, warm pink-red. Let this grass carry the show in a shade garden by partnering it with the green foliage of hostas, ferns, and other shade lovers. It looks beautiful with rock, too.

How to Grow
Same as *H. macra*. Less robust in growth than the green species, it is even slower to spread. If it begins to turn more green than yellow, move it to a sunnier spot.

Helictotrichon

hell-ik-toe-try´kun

Gramineae. Grass family

These clump-forming perennial grasses have arching leaf blades and rather sparse flowers held in narrow panicles. The genus includes about 30 species, most native to Eurasia, and 2 species native to alpine meadows and dry western prairies of North America.

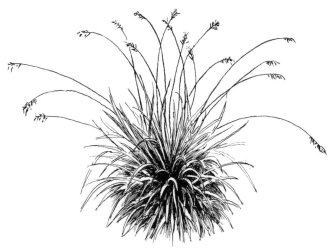

■ *sempervirens* *p. 143*
(Avena sempervirens; A. candida)
Blue oat grass
Zones 4–9. P/Cl/W
Height: 12–36 in., usually about 24 in. Spread: 12–24 in.

This clumping perennial is the same bright blue as blue Lyme grass (*Elymus arenarius* 'Glaucus') but is much better behaved in the garden. The spiky leaves are thin, only $1/8$–$3/8$ in. wide, and grow in dense tufts like a large version of blue fescue *(Festuca glauca)*. It doesn't flower much, especially in cold climates, but from the minute the leaves emerge in spring its foliage is an eye-catcher. Combine it in a foundation planting with a dwarf blue spruce and one of the dwarf blue-colored junipers, or contrast it with perennials of different habits and leaf shapes. Like other blue-gray grasses, it looks great with pink garden flowers.

How to Grow

Full or part sun. Needs well-drained soil to perform well, especially where winters are wet. Does best in a hot, sunny site. Develops the best blue color in dry soil. Pull out dead leaves as necessary, and cut back once a year. Divide older clumps in spring.

■ *sempervirens* 'Saphirsprundel' *p. 144*
'Saphirsprundel' ('Sapphire Fountain') blue oat grass
Zones 4–9. P/Cl/W
Height: 24 in. Spread: 24 in.

Like the species, but with even better clear blue-gray color. Its gently arching panicles rise above the stiff, evergreen leaves in late summer. A superb grass for the perennial border, either as a single accent or in groups as a transition. Try it with garden phlox of any color; white phlox will shine behind a planting of this cool-colored grass, which will also camouflage any mildewed foliage. This grass has extremely sharp-tipped, stiff foliage; work around it with care.

How to Grow
Same as *H. sempervirens.*

Hordeum

hor´dee-um
Gramineae. Grass family

These annual or perennial grasses have showy, bristly flower heads that can be highly ornamental in mass plantings. The genus includes about 20 species native to the north temperate zone, including the cereal grain barley *(Hordeum vulgare)* and many aggressive weedy grasses. The sharp flower spikes can be a danger to foraging animals, piercing mouths, eyes, and noses.

■ *jubatum* *p. 144*
Foxtail barley, squirreltail grass
Zones 4–10. PGA/C
Height: 12–30 in. Spread: 12–18 in.

A short-lived grass often grown as an annual for cut-flower arrangements or massed in informal gardens. It's utterly beautiful for several weeks in early summer when the feathery flower heads emerge. The nodding spikes are 4 in. long, and each floret is topped with a hairlike 3-in.-long awn. The flowers have a green and purple sheen that turns to beige as the "tail" puffs out and matures. Pick early for dried arrangements; discard any that show signs of falling apart. If you don't harvest or cut back the seed heads before they shatter, the grass will probably self-sow and may become weedy. Neither clumping nor running, foxtail barley grows like wheat: single-stemmed and lots of it.

This North American native is considered a pesky and dangerous weed in irrigated western pastures because the bristly seeds can injure foraging animals. If you live near grazing land, ranchers will thank you for not introducing it.

How to Grow
Full or part sun. Not fussy about soil or watering. Plant seeds in spring and grow as annual. Harvest or cut back seed heads before they shatter to prevent grass from self-sowing.

Hystrix
hi´stricks
Gramineae. Grass family

The botanical name of this genus is Greek for porcupine, an apt description for these grasses, whose seed heads bristle in all directions like porcupine quills — or like the bristles of a bottlebrush, their common name. They're perennials with loose tufts of leaves, and all share the typical bristly seed head. The six species are native to North America, China, New Zealand, and India.

■ *patula*   *p. 145*
Bottlebrush grass
Zones 4–9. P/Cl/W
Height: 24–48 in. Spread: 12–24 in.

This perennial American native is an interesting plant for a shady garden, thanks to its trademark bottlebrush seed heads, which persist from late summer through fall. In its natural haunts from Nova Scotia to North Dakota and south to Georgia, it occurs in and at the edge of woods. The foliage is unremarkable; the loose, upright tufts of $\frac{1}{4}$–$\frac{1}{2}$-in.-wide leaf blades bow near the top in a curly jumble, but above the leaves rise erect stems of bristled flower heads that catch the light, and the eye, in a shaded garden. The flower heads hold their florets close to the stem at first, but later open so that the bristles stick out at right angles. The flowers start green and ripen to beige above green leaves, which follow suit in late autumn. The grass makes an interesting counterpoint to the blue spires of the shade-loving American bellflower *(Campanula americana)*. For fresh arrangements, cut the flowers when they first emerge.

How to Grow
Full sun or part to moderate shade. Widely adaptable. Thrives in heavy clay as well as humusy soils and dry, rocky shade. Easy to grow from seed. Best for the naturalized garden. May self-sow and will readily populate a well-kept garden. Propagate by seed or division.

Imperata

im-per-ah´tuh
Gramineae. Grass family

A small group of perennial grasses, mostly from tropical climates. Of the eight species, one is a fast-spreading creeping grass, *I. cylindrica,* that was introduced to Florida as a forage grass. It is now classified as a noxious weed and cannot be sold in this country. A cultivated form of this grass, with striking red foliage, is a treasured ornamental.

■ *cylindrica* 'Red Baron' *p. 145*
(*I. cylindrica* var. *rubra*)
Japanese blood grass
Zones 6–9. P/R/W
Height: 12–18 in. Spread: 12 in.

Not as robust as the species, the mild-mannered 'Red Baron' is a welcome addition to the garden. It seldom if ever flowers and is grown for its bright red foliage. Leaves become flushed with garnet red as summer progresses, darkening into burgundy toward fall. Use it for an accent plant, especially on a west-facing lawn or ridge where it will be backlit by the setting sun. It also makes a colorful ribbon running along a lawn or edging a perennial border.

How to Grow
Full or part sun. Best in fertile, moist but well-drained soil. Propagate by division. Cut back once a year. If all-green shoots appear, it's a sign that the cultivar is reverting to its species type. Remove and destroy them immediately.

Juncus

jun´kus
Juncaceae. Rush family

Rushes have been appreciated for their usefulness as thatch, cordage, sandals, baskets, and other everyday products far longer than they've been admired by gardeners. Their botanical name has its root in the Latin *iugere,* to join, referring to the use of the stems in weaving and tying. In Japan, soft rush (*Juncus effusus*) is still cultivated for tatami, the woven mats that cover the floors of Japanese homes. These plants are also useful to animals in the wild. They are the favorite food of muskrat and moose and other creatures that frequent marshes, bogs, and other wet places. Ducks and migrating swallows seek out heavy stands of rushes for protective shelter. In the garden, rushes add a natural look to water features, blurring the transition from water to land.

■ *effusus* *p. 146*
(Juncus communis)
Soft rush, common rush, mat rush
Zones 4–9. P/Cl
Height: 18–48 in., usually about 24 in. Spread: 18–30 in.

This wayfaring rush occurs around the globe. Usually found in wet soil near water, it also grows in rich lowlands that are periodically flooded. Early European settlers in North America soon learned that the presence of this plant meant that the ground was too wet to cultivate crops.

The thin, cylindrical stems are dark green, almost black-green, and grow in a dense clump that spills outward from an erect center. The clump gradually expands by creeping roots. The foliage has a stiff look, but its stems are soft to the touch, and its flowers are a pretty addition. They sprout several inches down from the tips of the stems in nodding clusters of soft brown or gold. Each seed capsule contains innumerable minute seeds that look like dust. Soft rush makes an attractive plant in shallow water or at the edge of a pond. It turns golden in fall, then beige-brown in winter. Horizontally banded cultivars are available: 'Aureostriatus', with yellow bands; 'Vittatus', with narrow white bands; and 'Zebrinus', with broad white bands.

How to Grow
Sun to part or light shade. Grows most lush in rich, moist or wet soils or in shallow water, but is very adaptable. Tolerates dry soil in summer, but some stems may turn brown. Cut back old foliage in early spring, or let new stems grow up through old. May self-sow. Propagate by division; you can also grow from seed, but division yields a bigger plant faster.

■ *effusus* 'Spiralis' *p. 146*
(J. effusus var. spiralis)
Corkscrew rush
Zones 4–9. P/Cl
Height: 12–24 in. Spread: 12 in. or more

A curiosity for the water garden or container, this cultivar has curling stems that writhe every which way, like Medusa's hair. Clip some for arrangements and let the rest serve as a conversation piece or private poolside joke. The cultivar 'Curly Wurly' has even tighter spirals.

How to Grow
Part to light shade. Moist or wet soil; also shallow water. If you want to try it in a container, plant in a plastic pot and insert into a nondraining container filled with several inches of water, or keep on a saucer of water-filled gravel. Propagate by division.

■ *patens* p. 147
California gray rush
Zones 8–9. P/Cl
Height: 18–30 in. Spread: 18 in. or more

This rush has the typical spiky, cylindrical clump of stems, but it holds them more stiffly erect than soft rush. The flowers are brown bumbles held within the clump of stems. The foliage is a variable blue-gray-green and keeps its color year-round.

How to Grow

Sun to moderate shade. Very adaptable, but at its best in moist or wet fertile soil. Will also grow in shallow water. May be hardier than Zone 8; it hasn't been tried much outside of its native West Coast. Propagate by division. May self-sow. Cut back old foliage as needed.

Koeleria

koe-lair´ee-uh
Gramineae. Grass family

About 25 species of annual and perennial grasses with tufts of slender leaves and narrow spikes of flowers from the temperate regions of the Northern and Southern Hemispheres. Although the common name for the genus is hair grass, the coiffure varies considerably: some species are dense and lustrous, like a well-combed mane, and others look more like a cheap Beatles wig. Most grow in upright tufts. Some have blue-gray foliage. All are cool-season grasses that sport wands of showy flowers in late spring to summer, when the perennial garden is at its peak. Most of the ornamental species have a short life, lasting only one or two years in the garden.

■ *argentea* p. 147
Silver hair grass
Zones 6–9. P/Cl/C
Height: 12–18 in. Spread: 12–18 in.

Thick clumps of fine-textured, $\frac{1}{8}$–$\frac{1}{4}$-in.-wide leaves have a silvery cast that is more pronounced on the undersides of the leaves. This gives the plants a shimmering look, especially when they move in the breeze, like the flashing undersides of silver maple. The greenish white panicles of flowers bloom about the same time as Oriental poppies and irises and are smooth and glistening when they first emerge. They ripen to golden tan, still ornamental, although some gardeners prefer to clip them off so as not to detract from the grass's foliage. They are pretty flowers for dainty bouquets. Originally from the Himalayas.

How to Grow

Sun. Lean soils with excellent drainage. This grass sulks in shade, clay, and wet soils, but must have some moisture, although it is fairly drought-tolerant. A short-lived species that rarely lasts more than a couple of years in the garden. Cut back dormant foliage and wait for new cool-season growth. Propagate by seed or division.

■ *glauca* *p. 148*
(K. cristata var. *glauca)*
Large blue hair grass
Zones 6–9. P/Cl/C
Height: 6–24 in., usually about 12 in. Spread: 6–12 in.

Dainty next to most grasses, it grows in a dense mound of thin leaves that flash blue-gray. Wands of flowers cover the plant for several weeks in late spring to summer. The clump may include mature whitish tan panicles as well as glossy green ones just emerging.

How to Grow

Same as *K. argentea*. This small grass is easy to fit into a perennial border, although it will be short-lived in the moist, fertile soil usually found there. It does best in infertile, sandy, alkaline soil.

■ *macrantha* *p. 148*
Crested hair grass, June grass
Zones 2–9. P/Cl/C
Height: 12–18 in. Spread: 12 in.

This tufted perennial grass grows in erect, compact clumps. Its leaves are usually tinged with gray-green, although the intensity of the color may vary. The narrow spikes of flowers provide good vertical line, especially when the grass is used in mass plantings. Since it self-sows readily, it's best to keep it out of the border. Plant it in a naturalistic meadow, with wildflowers like black-eyed Susans and yarrow, or put it in a group with other grasses. It also looks good with native western drylands plants, such as artemisias and desert marigold, or with Mediterranean herbs, including oregano and billowy blue catmint.

How to Grow

Sun. Lean, light soil with excellent drainage; rocky or gravelly soil. Thrives in drought and intense sun, but declines in moist, fertile soil and in shade. A good grass for a naturalistic western desert landscape. Cut back if dead foliage is disagreeable to you, or let new green leaves come up through the old clump. Scatter seed for a meadow planting, or propagate by division. Self-sows.

Lagurus

la-gur´us
Gramineae. Grass family
   The only species is described below.

■ *ovatus* *p. 149*
Hare's tail
All zones. A/W
Height: 12–24 in. Spread: 6–12 in.
   The oval panicles of this annual grass are as white and furry as bunny tails. (The genus name comes from the Greek *lagos*, hare, and *oura*, tail.) The soft foliage is also a pleasure to stroke, but the loose tuft of green leaves usually goes unnoticed once the flower heads spring up. Plant this summer bloomer in your annual garden with wiry-stemmed red field poppies or with stout, colorful zinnias, or grow it for cutting. Clip the flowers when young for long-lasting decorations in dried arrangements. Plant grows like wheat: lots of single stems.

How to Grow
Sun. Light, very well drained soil; also does well in average garden soil. Sow seed in spring where you want the plants to grow. Self-sows but never to pest status.

Luzula

loo-zoo´luh
Juncaceae. Rush family
   In the same family as the familiar pond and marsh rushes, the 80 or so species in this genus are mostly native to woodlands rather than wet places. Their flat, grasslike leaves are often soft and hairy, and they grow in tufts or loose, low mounds. In the wild they look just like clumps of grass among the leaves of the forest floor. All perennials, they are good, underused plants that deserve more attention in the shade or woodland garden. They combine beautifully with violets and spring ephemeral wildflowers as well as the more usual hostas and ferns. Most are native to Eurasia, but some are native to North America, and others are naturalized here.

■ *nivea* 'Snowbird' *p. 149*
'Snow Bird' snowy wood rush
Zones 4–9. P/Cl
Height: 8–12 in. Spread: 8–12 in.
   The showiest of the wood rushes, this perennial bears abundant clusters of lovely white flowers above its thin gray

leaves. The clump of foliage is soft to the touch, thanks to the velvety hairs on the leaves, which collect dew in shining silver droplets along their edges. 'Snow Bird' looks great against the deep tones and round leaves of ornamental foliage heucheras such as 'Palace Purple' and 'Pewter Veil'. The species form of this cultivar has ivory-colored flowers that mature to soft beige and is beautiful with wild blue phlox *(Phlox stolonifera* and *P. divaricata).*

How to Grow
Part to light shade. Best in moist, humusy soil. Propagate from division, or grow from seed (not all seedlings will be exactly like the parent cultivar). Cut back spent flowers and foliage as needed.

Melica
mel' ih-kuh
Gramineae. Grass family
Melic grasses are tall clumping grasses, medium to fine in foliage texture, with varying types of inflorescences. Some are narrow and dense, others are soft and fluffy or strictly one-sided, and some have shimmering, open panicles with a light, rhythmic beauty. The 60 or so species, all perennials, hail from Eurasia, North Africa, and other temperate regions. Many are western North American natives. The genus name probably refers to the sweet sap of *Melica nutans* and may come from the Italian *miele,* meaning honey.

■ *altissima* 'Atropurpurea'
Purple Siberian melic
Zones 4–9. P/Cl/C
Height: 8 in. Spread: 8 in.
The cultivar name of this clump-forming, cool-season perennial refers to the flowers, not the foliage. Its $3/8$–$3/4$-in.-wide leaves are green, with a slight gloss, and grow in a low clump. Flowers arise on tall bare stems that can quiver as much as 2 ft. above the foliage, with delicate, open panicles that take on a tawny purplish hue. The species is from Siberia, and this cultivar has an innate preference for cool climates and an aversion to hot sun and dry soil. Try it in a lightly shaded or moist-soil perennial border or in a shade garden. Because of its low foliage, you can use it as a see-through plant; its slender flowering stems won't obscure plants behind it. The delicate, early-blooming flowers are charming with salvias and other small-flowered perennials.

How to Grow
Part shade; keep it out of direct sun in hot-summer regions. Moist, humusy, very well drained soil; dig in a generous amount of compost, leaf mold, or rotted manure to lighten heavier soils. Cut back spent flowering stalks and dormant foliage. Self-sows, but seedlings may not be like the parent plant. Propagate by division.

■ *ciliata* p. 150
Hairy melic grass, silky spike melic
Zones 5–8. P/Cl/C
Height: 8–12 in. Spread: 8–12 in.

This perennial cool-season grass grows in tufts of gray-green foliage, but you'll never notice the leaves once the flowers appear in late spring or early summer. The cylindrical spikes are pale, creamy tan, with silky white hairs as soft-looking as down. Erect at first, they settle into a slight nodding posture. They are just as decorative in arrangements as in an informal garden, where the flowers can lean about in a casual way and collapse comfortably. If you want them to stay at attention, wrap a circlet of wire around them.

How to Grow
Sun to part shade; keep out of full sun in hot-summer areas. Moist but well-drained soil of good fertility. Cut back after the flowers are spent and the foliage is dormant. Propagate by seed or division.

Milium

mil'ee-um
Gramineae. Grass family

The flat-bladed leaves of the annual or perennial millet grasses grow in medium-tall relaxed tussocks. Only one of the six species in this genus is grown as an ornamental, and usually in the yellow variegated form. In its species form, it is found in moist or rocky woods from Nova Scotia to Minnesota and south to Maryland, as well as in Eurasia.

■ *effusum* 'Aureum'
Golden wood millet, Bowles' golden grass
Zones 6–9. P/Cl/C
Height: 12–24 in. Spread: 12–24 in. or more

This cool-season perennial grass has glorious yellow-green foliage that spills over in an arching mound of flat, $\frac{1}{4}$–$\frac{1}{2}$-in.-wide leaves. It spreads at a slow to moderate rate by creeping roots but is never a pest. Planted in shade or a

wooded setting, golden wood millet lights up the garden like a pool of sunlight on the woodland floor. The young leaves have the strongest yellow coloring; they become green-yellow as the season progresses. When backlit by afternoon sun, the translucent foliage comes alive. Delicate open sprays of flowers rise well above the grassy foliage in late spring to early summer and quiver in a shimmering haze with every breeze. After flowering, the plant may decline a bit. The foliage is evergreen in mild climates.

Bowles' golden grass is beautiful with the usual ferns and hostas, but for something special, try combining it with the buttery cupped flowers and deep green foliage of celandine poppy *(Stylophorum diphyllum)* and the flowering, bare brown branches of yellow Cornelian cherry *(Cornus mas)*.

How to Grow
Light to moderate shade. Moist but well-drained, humusy soil rich in organic matter; also does well on a rocky, woodsy slope and adapts to average garden soil in shade. Cut back spent flowers and tired foliage. To propagate, slice off divisions with a sharp spade or start from fresh seed; most of the seedlings will come true to color. May self-sow moderately.

Miscanthus
mis-kan´thus
Gramineae. Grass family

The premiere genus of ornamental grasses, and rightly so. Unfussy about soil and conditions, these robust perennials grow in sturdy clumps, providing backbone in the landscape and adapting to a multitude of uses, from hedges to poolside greenery to specimen plantings. Some have wide banners of leaves; others finer, arching foliage. All sport showy plumes of flowers that can persist for months in the garden and even longer in dried arrangements. It's a pleasure to watch the flowers emerge and mature; they have a satin gloss and often beautiful pink, red, or purple coloring when new, and then gradually soften to fluffy heads delightful to touch. Even when the seeds have blown away, the bare, curled stems of the inflorescence remain appealing. In the winter garden, miscanthus grasses add structure and beauty, as well as delightful rustling noises and movement.

There are 17 species of miscanthus, but dozens of fine cultivars have been selected. These versatile grasses are native to the Old World tropics, Southeast Asia, and South Africa. Many ornamental cultivars have been developed by plant breeders in Germany. Some ornamental grass suppliers list the plants by their German names; others use English translations. Where appropriate, both are provided in these plant descriptions.

■ *floridulus* *p. 150*
(M. *sinensis* var. *giganteus*; M. *japonicus*)
Giant Chinese silver grass
Zones 5–9. P/Cl/W
Height: 8–12 ft. or more. Spread: 36 in. or more

A big grass, sometimes misidentified as M. 'Giganteus', with arching leaves up to $1\frac{1}{2}$ in. wide and stout stems up to 2 in. in diameter. Stems grow strongly erect from the base of the clump and hold the grass upright even in wind. The flowers appear in early to midfall and are a bonanza in areas with long growing seasons. They're silky at first, with a reddish sheen, and then feather out into fluffy pyramidal plumes held a foot or more above the foliage. Like all miscanthus flowers, they're beautiful in fresh or dried arrangements. The grass goes dormant in fall. The leaves first turn purplish red over tan, then gradually drop from the culms by midwinter, leaving a structural accent of vertical stems.

This giant can be the center of attention in a mixed border or grouping. Its lush foliage complements other large plants, such as plume poppy (*Macleaya cordata*), cup plant (*Silphium perfoliatum*), and hibiscus, including the wild red mallow (*Hibiscus coccineus*). It also makes a good hedge or windbreak and is a fine anchor for a group of mixed grasses. Leaves tend to die off near the base of the plant, leaving it with a bare-legged look. If you find this unappealing, plant shorter grasses.

How to Grow

Sun. Moist but well-drained soil. Reaches its best height in moist soil, but adapts to average garden conditions. Consider the site carefully before you plant; this tough-rooted grass will soon be impossible to remove without the aid of heavy equipment. Stays in a very slowly enlarging clump. Cut back old stems in early spring; by summer, it will be a dense waterfall of wide green leaves.

■ *oligostachyus*
(*M. oligostachys*)
Small Japanese silver grass
Zones 5–9. P/Cl/W
Height: 3–4 ft. Spread: 2 ft.

This Japanese native is as diminutive as a miscanthus gets, being only knee-high. It's also less dense, growing in narrow, vertical clumps that need no staking to stay in good form. Its erect flowers, a beautiful pinkish silver, are borne in late summer. It's a good grass for a place of honor in the perennial border, and an attention-getter in groups or in masses. Combine it with 'Purple Dome' fall asters and other late-blooming perennials of contrasting mounded form, or carpet the ground at its feet with low-growing lamb's-ears. The grass mellows to soft tan in winter.

How to Grow

Sun. Well-drained average garden soil. Cut back old foliage in early spring. Propagate by division.

■ *sacchariflorus* *p. 151*
Silver banner grass
Zones 5–9. P/R/W
Height: 4–8 ft. Spread: 2–3 ft. or more

Unlike most, this miscanthus species grows by creeping rhizomes, spreading especially fast in wet areas. This grass is a native of wetlands in Japan, China, and other places, and it's happiest in moist soils. That makes it an excellent choice for edging a pond or adding interest to a wet meadow. It has wide leaves, up to ³/₄ in. across, that thrust strongly upward and then arch over. The late-summer flowers are soft silver when they emerge and fluff out to white whiskbrooms; they're a little narrower than the spreading feathery flowers of the familiar *M. sinensis,* and they stand upright, well above the foliage. Like other miscanthus flowers, they can tell you at a glance which way the wind blows, since they eventually stiffen in a posture with the plumes turned away from prevailing winds. The grass turns warm yellow to golden tan in fall and winter, and the flowers stay attractive for months.

How to Grow
Sun. Moist to wet soils. In dry soils or clay, it spreads more slowly and isn't as lush. Choose a site carefully; it is aggressive. Keep it out of perennial borders, and plant it where it can roam. Cut back old foliage in early spring. Propagate by division.

■ *sinensis* *(see below for photos)*
Eulalia grass, Japanese silver grass
Zones 5–9. P/Cl/W
Height: 3–12 ft., depending on cultivar. Spread: 3 ft. or more

The old man of ornamental grasses, Eulalia has been a garden favorite for centuries. Ancient clumps still thrive in front of American Victorian houses. This warm-season perennial grows in large clumps. Its leaves grow up then out, in a cascade of graceful foliage. The flowers are a superb second act. They arise in summer to fall, gleaming like silk, then fluff out into showy sprays above the foliage. The grass turns various shades of gold and tan in fall, with occasional russet overtones. Its foliage holds up well even in snowy climates.

Adaptable and versatile, this grass grows well in almost any garden and in most combinations. Dense foliage makes it a good backdrop for perennial flowers, and it adds pizzazz to plantings of shrubs and evergreens. It's a standard in waterside gardens and in mixed-grass groupings. A row or group of miscanthus also makes a neighbor-friendly hedge.

Dozens of easy-to-grow cultivars are now available, and new ones are appearing all the time. The listings here include many of the long-time favorites, as well as a sampling of the best new cultivars. Unless otherwise noted, the cultivars grow well in Zones 5–9.

How to Grow

Sun; will also grow in part shade but tends to be floppy there. Average soil. Cut back old foliage in early spring. Propagate by division, if you can; these plants are tough-rooted and many cultivars are hard to divide even with an axe.

'Bluetenwunder' forms a tight, erect clump that reaches about 5 ft. Foliage is strongly vertical, not arching significantly even at the tips. Small plumes of flowers bloom in late summer. Be careful working around this grass; the leaf edges are sharp enough to slice an ungloved hand. It is hardy to Zone 4.

'Burgunder' ('Burgundy') is a slim miscanthus that grows to 4 ft. The thin, curling leaves give it an airy look, and their unusual deep-red flushed color is beautiful with pink or yellow perennials as well as with white-flowered phlox, salvias, and with annuals such as multiflora petunias. Zones 7–9.

'Cabaret' is a tall (6–8 ft.) variegated cultivar with cool green and white foliage. The broad ribbons of almost inch-wide leaves, white in the middle with green edges, grow in a weeping cascade. 'Cabaret' blooms in early fall, with straight stems of pink flowers that lighten to soft creamy white. Foliage turns tan in winter. Variegated forms of miscanthus are elegant with white-flowering perennials, but they also look good with almost any other color. They're particularly effective partners for blazing reds. Try this grass with scarlet salvia *(Salvia splendens)* or shrublike, red-flowered pineapple sage *(S. elegans)*, or let it add a cool backdrop to a raised pot of flaming red geraniums. It grows in Zones 7–10. (See photo on p. 151.)

'Cosmopolitan' is a variegated cultivar of imposing stature thanks to its girth of 4–5 ft. and broad leaves that spill over like a handful of wide ribbons. From a distance, the foliage looks cool gray-green; up close, you can see that the effect is created by white edgings on each green leaf. Abundant plumes of flowers emerge coppery red and are held high above the foliage. This is a fabulous specimen plant that needs no staking and is excellent in warm climates. (See photo on p. 152.)

'Flamingo' is a lush, elegant grass with huge pink plumes. Put it in a place of honor as a specimen or along water, where its mirrored image can double the glory. (See photo on p. 152.)

'Gold Feather' ('Goldfeder') has foliage of an unusual lime green edged with gold bands. Less robust than most cultivars but worth patience until it's large enough to make a splash. Grows 5–6 ft. tall.

'Gracillimus', or maiden grass, is one of the most delicate cultivars but also one of the hardiest (Zone 5). A longtime garden favorite, it has narrow leaves that grow in a wide, arching clump up to 8 ft. tall. It may collapse under the weight of its own foliage and flowers, and it will certainly bow beneath snow unless you support it with a sturdy loop of wire. It blooms late, in midfall. The silken tassels are rich copper-red at first and mellow to silvery white. Foliage turns warm tan in winter. (See photo on p. 153.) 'Gracillimus Nana' is a miniature form with even finer foliage. At 3–4 ft. tall, it makes an excellent choice for smaller gardens. Can be slow to become established.

'Graziella' is a slender-leaved, early-blooming miscanthus that reaches about 6 ft. high and 3 ft. wide. Large white flowers, held well above the foliage, appear in summer. The wide swords of iris leaves will look even more emphatic beside this cultivar's slender foliage, and pure white shasta daisies are lovely with this grass. Hardy to Zone 5. (See photo on p. 153.)

'Kascade' is an early-blooming cultivar providing a long display in Zones 5–8. Growing 5–7 ft. tall and 3–4 ft. wide, it raises its pink flowers in summer, and they soon spill over of their own weight, washing down the plant in a gleaming wave of silver-pink. It's a glorious plant for the mixed border or as a specimen grouping, and it's unbeatable near water. (See photo on p. 154.)

'Little Fountain' ('Kleine Fontaine') is a compact cultivar of 3–4 ft. in height with an extra-long flower show. Rather than coming all at once, its blooms push up over a period of weeks, producing a continuous fountain of flowers over the green leaves. Its compact form makes it an excellent choice in front of taller grasses or in the mid-ground of the border. (See photo on p. 154.)

'Morning Light', a relatively new cultivar, is a smaller version (4–5 ft.) of 'Gracillimus'. Its silver-striped, fine-textured leaves glisten in the wind, giving it a light, airy feeling in the garden that's just like the old favorite. In early to midfall, deep pink-bronze flowers push up, then lighten to oatmeal white. It is beautiful by itself or in groups and looks great with the heavier branches of woody shrubs, such as 'Arnold Promise' witch hazel, or with the glossy leaves of bayberry and other broad-leaved evergreens. Light pink wands of coral bells and feathery astilbes are enchanting against the shimmery foliage of this grass. Hardy to Zone 5. (See photo on p. 155.)

'Purpurascens', or flame grass, earns its name in fall, when the red-tinged foliage changes to a beautiful red-orange. It holds good color into winter, gradually deepening to burgundy. A compact, upright grower, 4–5 ft. tall, it expands gradually by spreading rhizomes. Grows well in light shade, though fall foliage will be lighter and less vivid. Its hardiness is in dispute, with recommendations ranging from Zone 7 as far north as Zone 4. (See photo on p. 155.) 'Hercules' has a similar erect habit and warm reddish gold foliage in fall. It reaches 3–5 ft. tall and is hardy to Zone 4. (Both cultivars may be listed as *M. oligostachyus*.) Try either of them with a clump of flaking cinnamon-barked river birch and a bevy of purple autumn crocus at its feet, or combine with ornamental junipers and other small conifers with interesting color.

'Sarabande' is an excellent hardy cultivar (to Zone 4) similar to the popular 'Gracillimus', with finely textured foliage touched with silver for an extra-light effect. Contrast it with a mass of deep green coltsfoot *(Tussilago farfara)* at its feet, or plant it in the border with perennials such as hardy geraniums, salvias, or glistening pink and white mallows.

'Silver Feather' ('Silberfeder') grows to 9 ft. with a spread of 4 ft. or more and is hardy to Zone 5. Early in the season it presents a flared arch of fresh green foliage, followed in summer by large plumes of silver flowers held high above the foliage. (See photo on p. 156.)

'Silver Spider' ('Silberspinne') is another narrow-leaved cultivar that tops out at 4–5 ft. The fine-textured foliage has a silvery lightness. In late summer, it blooms with spidery tassels that are reddish at first and then turn silver. Grows in Zones 5–9.

'Siren' ('Sirene') has possibly the best flowers of any miscanthus, raising an abundance of extravagant plumes high above the 5–6-ft.-tall foliage. An excellent specimen and beautiful along water. Grows in Zones 5–9.

'Strictus', or porcupine grass, is an old favorite and still valuable in today's gardens. (It may also be listed as *M. sinensis* var. *strictus*.) It flourishes in light or part shade in hot summer climates and will also grow in wet soil or in shallow water. It forms a substantial vertical clump (6–8 ft. tall and 3–5 ft. wide) of sharply pointed leaves, with some sticking out at 45° angles like a pelt of sharp quills. Light yellow horizontal bands mark the leaves with an effect like dappled sunlight. New leaves are green and acquire the typical coloring as they mature. This grass is often confused with *M. sinensis*

'Zebrinus', zebra grass, which has the same yellow bands but a habit that is arching and graceful rather than rigidly upright and prickly. Porcupine grass foliage is interesting in fresh arrangements. It quickly turns tan in cold weather.

'Undine' is a slender-stemmed cultivar with pretty silver flowers and warm fall color. It grows to only 4 ft., a good size in the smaller garden, the perennial border, or as a transition between taller grasses and ground covers. Grows in Zones 5–9. (See photo on p. 156.)

'Variegatus', one of the oldest variegated cultivars, can still be found in "grandma's gardens," often with another old-timer, ribbon grass *(Phalaris arundinacea* var. *picta).* An outstanding garden grass, it grows to a substantial height and width (6–9 ft. high and 4–5 ft. wide) and has creamy striped foliage that looks ghostly white at a distance. It is beautiful in the perennial garden or along water, and the color brightens any group of mixed green grasses. Though often planted with black-eyed Susans, its cool color is a better foil for red, pink, blue, purple, and white flowers. A nice partner for Siberian irises. Prone to collapse, even without the weight of the abundant pink flowers that bloom in early fall; give it a sturdy loop of wire for support. Thrives in part or light shade. Give it some afternoon shade where summers are hot. Grows in Zones 6–9. (See photo on p. 157.)

'Yaku Jima' looks like a downsized version of *M. sinensis* 'Gracillimus'. Not only smaller (3–4 ft.) than other miscanthuses, it also has narrower leaves. Abundant buffy flowers bloom in summer and are usually held above the foliage. (See photo on pp. 48–49.) Newer Yaku Jima–type cultivars have improved on the standard. 'Adagio', one of the most compact, is perfect for a smaller mixed bed or border. The flowers stretch high above the compact clump, and in fall the leaves turn a rich coppery bronze.

'Zebrinus' or Zebra grass, like porcupine grass *(M. sinensis* var. *strictus),* has horizontal yellow bands speckling the foliage and grows to the same height (6–8 ft.) but in wide (to 6 ft.) arching mounds that have a tendency to collapse without a little support from the gardener. Young leaves lack the yellow bands at first but develop them as they mature. Fluffy pinkish flowers bloom in fall. An old favorite, it's a good grass for garden or water's edge. (See photo on p. 157.)

■ *transmorrisonensis* *p. 158*
Evergreen miscanthus
Zones 7–10. P/Cl/W
Height: 3–4 ft. Spread: 3 ft.

The unusual evergreen habit of this warm-season grass and its small size have some taxonomists arguing for its status as a separate species. Others say it belongs with *M. sinensis*. A recent introduction from Taiwan, it grows in dense arching clumps of narrow green leaves and bears reddish flowers that ripen to warm tawny gold. It stays evergreen in mild climates and blooms in spring. In cold climates it blooms in early to midsummer. Flowers are held high above the foliage, but cascade out from the plant in an arching curve.

How to Grow
Same as *M. sinensis*.

Molinia
mo-lin´ee-uh
Gramineae. Grass family

These clumping perennial grasses have soft, narrow leaves and loose flower heads. There are only two or three species, native to bogs of Europe and Asia, including the open moors, which is where they get the common name, moor grass. Purple moor grass *(Molinia caerulea)* is sometimes found growing wild in limited areas of the eastern states.

These grasses have never achieved the popularity of the miscanthus tribe, but they're equally valuable in the garden and as carefree, although a bit more persnickety about soil conditions, preferring an acidic soil. Moor grasses are natural companions with heaths, heathers, and Scotch broom, but they also look at home with perennial flowers, shrubs, and conifers. Try them against a dark background to accentuate the delicate flowers, especially when they take on warm autumn tones. Once you discover their beauty, you won't be able to resist adding them to your garden.

■ *caerulea* *(see below for photo)*
Purple moor grass
Zones 4–9. P/Cl/W
Height: 1–3 ft. Spread: 2–3 ft.

Don't let this low-mounding grass fool you — when it's in bloom it reaches for the sky, shooting stalks of airy flowers

6–7 ft. into the air. The "purple" *(caerulea)* in the name is a little misleading; its only trace is in new flowers, but they may also be brown or tan, and at any rate, they quickly lose any purple sheen as they ripen to tawny gold.

This warm-season perennial grass has a bold presence, yet because of the see-through quality of the bare flower stems and airy panicles, it's lightweight enough to use in a mixed border. It also looks dramatic with rocks or on a hillside with artemisias, perovskia, and other shrublike plants. Or mingle a small group of them with heathers.

'Heidebraut' ('Heather Bride') has dense, compact clumps of leaves, and flower stems that mostly stand erect, offering excellent vertical line with the grace of transparent flowers. The stems and spikelets are a warm tawny gold in color, and the flowers are abundant. (See photo on p. 158.)

'Moorflamme' is an outstanding compact cultivar for cooler climates. Foliage reaches 1–2 ft. high and turns orange-red in fall with deeper notes of purple. Its flowers emerge dark purple-brown.

How to Grow
Sun or very light shade. Does best in moist, acidic soil. Will also grow in clay and sandy soil and will tolerate some dryness. Foliage and flowers eventually fall on their own, breaking off at the base of the stem; clip off any straggling foliage in early spring. This grass requires some patience to get started from a small division; give it two or even three years to reach its full glory in the garden. Once it flowers, it may self-sow, but seedlings take several years to reach a good size. Propagate by slicing off 4–6-in. divisions from mature plants.

■ *caerulea* ssp. *litorialis* *p. 159*
(Molinia litorialis; M. caerulea ssp. *arundinacea)*
Tall moor grass
Zones 5–8. P/Cl/W
Height: 2–3 ft. Spread: 2–3 ft.
 Stalks of this taller version of purple moor grass shoot up to heights of 6–9 ft., carrying the flowers like a burst of fireworks above the low-growing foliage. Flowers and foliage turn warm yellow in fall, then soften to golden tan for winter. Like other moor grasses, this tall one's slender flower stalks make it easy to place in the mixed border. They won't obscure plants behind them or shade those in front.

'Skyracer', an even taller selection, can reach 6–8 ft. when in flower. Its slim but strong straight stems make it an excellent architectural accent in the garden. Turns rich buttery yellow in fall. (See photo on p. 159.)

'Staefa' is a hardier (Zones 4–9) and shorter version of tall moor grass, its flowers reaching only 4–5 ft., roughly half the height of the tallest cultivars. The foliage is more weeping in habit and turns a lovely warm yellow in fall.

One of the most delicate moor grasses, 'Transparent' has fragile flower heads that rise to a hazy cloud at a height of 5–6 ft. It is a fine-textured sparkler in the garden or along a small pool.

How to Grow
Same as *M. caerulea*.

Muhlenbergia

mew-len-ber´jee-uh
Gramineae. Grass family

These mostly American, mostly perennial grasses differ so much in appearance from species to species that only a botanist can tell they're all related. Some are low and creeping, with narrow flowering spikes; others are arching clumps with clouds of flowers. Of the 125 or so species, all but about eight are native to the West, Southwest, and Mexico; the rest hail from southern Asia.

Many of the muhly grasses are valuable forage on the western range. The recent interest in native American plants, however, has made growers and gardeners take a closer look at their ornamental possibilities. With their natural adaptation to the rigorous western climate, especially the excellent drought tolerance of many species, they could become future garden favorites in the West. As these grasses are tried in garden settings, they may turn out to be adaptable to gardens in other areas of the country as well.

■ *dumosa* *p. 160*
Bamboo muhly
Zones 8–10. P/R/C
Height: 3–9 ft., usually 3–6 ft. Spread: 3 ft. or more

This unusual grass looks like a miniature fine-textured bamboo. Its leaves start out solidly sheathed around the wiry, woody stems, then branch and rebranch at the middle and upper nodes, forming cascades of foliage. The flowers are borne at the tips of the branches, and though not especially showy, they give a golden glow to the arching clump.

Like its namesake, bamboo muhly expands its territory by creeping rhizomes, but it's nowhere near as pushy. A native of the desert Southwest, it thrives in dry soils, although it will grow taller with more moisture. Plant it wherever you want to give a lush look to a dry garden, or where you need a graceful, filmy accent. It also takes well to large pots, where it can spill over the sides.

How to Grow
Sun. Well-drained ordinary soil. Also does well in dry and rocky or sandy soil. Sulks in heavy clay; lighten those soils with plenty of sand or grow in pots instead. Excellent drought tolerance. Propagate by dividing the scaly rhizomes.

■ *filipes*
Purple muhly
Zones 7–9. P/Cl/W
Height: 18–24 in. Spread: 12–18 in.

Ethereal in flower, this grass produces gauzy clouds similar in effect to purple love grass, though taller. The flowers create a filmy mass 2–4 ft. above the foliage, in mid- to late fall. It's a wonder to watch the panicle of flowers emerge and change from its narrow, dark purple beginnings to its final cloud of glory. The rest of the season, purple muhly is a quiet clump of tufted leaves. This American native comes from moist pine barrens along the Gulf and southeastern Atlantic coasts. It's showy in masses. Slip a few plants into a border for late-season splendor, or try it with a background of needled or broad-leaved evergreens.

How to Grow
Sun to light shade. Moist, well-drained soil. Does especially well in moist sand and in rocky, light soils. Grows well in gardens near the coast.

■ *pubescens* *p. 160*
Soft blue Mexican muhly
Zones 9–10. P/Cl/C
Height: 8–12 in. Spread: 8–12 in.

This is one of many perennial muhly grasses worth a try in the garden. Although it lacks the flowering clouds of *M. filipes*, it does have a commendable neatly mounded habit and lovely soft foliage. The moderately narrow ¼–⅜-in.-wide leaves are an excellent blue-green color, and their downy hairs catch every drop of dew for a bejeweled effect. As cold weather approaches, the foliage takes on a reddish tinge. It dies back in cold winters. The soft spikes of late-spring-blooming flowers are held above the foliage. They are an appealing gray-blue with a hint of purple and look pretty in a small bouquet as well as in the garden. Plant in groups or singly in a dry, naturalistic landscape, or combine it with sage *(Salvia officinalis)*, lavender, and other Mediterranean plants of complementary colors and contrasting textures.

How to Grow
Sun to part shade. Well-drained, light soils, including sandy and rocky soil. Good plant for coastal gardens. May self-sow. Propagate by seed or division. Like other plants recently introduced to gardens, the full extent of the hardiness and tolerance of this grass is not yet known. Its native habitat is in mountain cliffs and canyons of Mexico; it may be cold-tolerant farther north than Zone 9.

■ *rigens*   *p. 161*
Deer grass
Zones 7–9. P/Cl/C
Height: 2–4 ft. Spread: 3 ft.
   This cool-season perennial grass grows in dense clumps of slender, gray-green leaves. Unlike other cool-season types, it stays green right through summer, even in the driest gardens. The slim flower spikes are packed with tiny seeds and lack the hairlike awns that give the flowers of other muhlys a feathery softness. Try it in a naturalistic dry garden of lemon marigold, artemisias, and euphorbias, or as a ground cover on a slope for cool-looking cover in hot summer. Used for basket-making. In the San Francisco Bay area, it is grown as accent in industrial sites, especially the Hewlett-Packard facilities. Nice alternative to pampas grass in California.

How to Grow
Full sun to part shade. Widespread in its natural western range, it grows just about anywhere except in waterlogged soils. Does best in moist soil, but its deep roots can plumb underground water. Also tolerates alkaline and saline soils.

Oryzopsis
(Orysopsis)
or-ee-zop´sis
Gramineae. Grass family
   Mostly perennial grasses of slender tufting habit and narrow or open panicles, depending on the species. The genus includes about 35 or so species from North America and Eurasia. The American species are mostly western natives; a few are native to the East and some more widespread. The botanical name comes from the Greek *oryza,* rice, and *opsis,* appearance, and alludes to the resemblance to true rice *(Oryza sativa).* The leaves and seeds make good forage for wild and ranch grazers, and the seeds were once an important food to Native Americans.

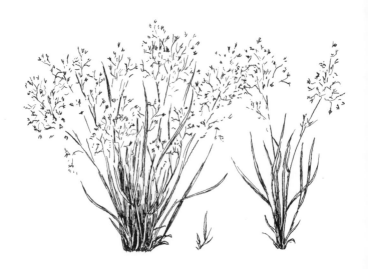

■ *hymenoides* *p. 161*
Indian rice grass, Indian millet, silkgrass
Zones 7–10. P/Cl/C
Height: 12–30 in. Spread: 12–24 in.

A beautiful airy grass with fine-textured foliage and vibrant, delicate open panicles of small seeds. The inflorescences are intriguing at close range: the silky-tufted seeds are held on thin wiry stems that kink and curve. In the wild, it was once common from Mexico through Texas and the desert West, as well as in the Canadian plains from Manitoba to British Columbia. Like many native plants, it has been decimated by grazing, development, and replacement by invasive alien species.

A cool-season perennial, it's at its best in spring; by early summer it is dormant tan, although the clump remains standing into winter. In a low-water garden, where plants go dormant in hot summer, it looks like a natural part of the cycle. Plant with flowering drought-tolerant perennials and silver-foliaged plants. It's a great grass for fresh or dried arrangements.

How to Grow
Sun. Flourishes in dry soils akin to those of its natural desert and plains habitat. Also grows in ordinary, very well drained garden soil. Adapted to extremely dry desert conditions, it fails to thrive if given too much water in summer. Propagate by seed. May self-sow. Limits of cold tolerance are yet to be established; it may grow in colder regions than Zone 7.

Panicum

pan´ih-kum

Gramineae. Grass family

A diverse genus of annual and perennial species, between 500 and 600 worldwide. Many are North American natives, including the excellent ornamental switch grass *(P. virgatum)*, one of the dominant species of the tallgrass prairie that once blanketed the middle of the continent. The common name of the genus, panic grass, is derived from *Panicum*, a Latin name for millet. (*Panicum miliaceum* is white proso millet, a common ingredient in birdseed mixes.)

Panic grasses generally grow in a luxuriant clump of long leaves and have gloriously light and airy panicles of flowers. A plethora of new cultivars, and others that were developed in grass-appreciating Germany, are becoming available to American gardeners. Translations of the German cultivar names are included in the descriptions below; plants may be listed in catalogs and references in either or both languages.

■ *clandestinum*

Deer tongue grass

Zones 4–9. P/Cl/W

Height: 1–4 ft. Spread: 2–3 ft.

At first glance, this warm-season grass looks nothing like a *Panicum*. Its leaves are short and wide and stick out from the stem at sharp angles every few inches like a bamboo. When it blooms, though, you can see the family resemblance. The flowers are pretty panicles at the tip of each stem, and the airy seed heads last for months. The slightly furry stems of this grass are reddish brown and contrast beautifully with the bright green, inch-wide leaves. In the wild, deer tongue grass grows in woods and at wood's edge. Its stems may grow erect or stretch laxly along the ground, especially after blooming. Leaves begin to emerge in early spring, and the fresh, light green foliage is appealing with spring ephemeral wildflowers or with bulbs. It's also a beautiful contrast to lacy or leathery ferns, and it looks as good as a small bamboo along streams and water. Plant in masses in a shade or woodland garden or edge paths to create a wide swathe of beautiful yellow fall color.

How to Grow

Part sun to moderate shade. Leaves are deeper green in shade; they tend to look sickly yellowish in full sun. Moist, humusy soil is best, but it will also grow well in heavier soils. Does well in humid, hot summers. Support the clump with a loop of wire to keep it erect when flowering. It dies back in winter and needs no cutting back.

■ *virgatum*   *p. 162*
Switch grass
Zones 5–9. P/Cl/W
Height: 3–7 ft. Spread: 2–3 ft.

Spectacular in flower, this perennial grass grows in narrow, erect clumps. Some plants may have leaves with a decided curl, while others are rigidly erect. Either way, the cloud of flowers creates an eye-catching contrast atop the vertical column of foliage. The slender leaves, 1–2 ft. long, are medium green in summer, turning bright yellow, gold, or orange in fall. Flower panicles open dark reddish purple to silvery white in midsummer, forming an airy mass 12–16 in. above the foliage that mellows to beige in fall.

This North American native is well adapted to the vagaries of our climate and tolerates both wet and dry sites. A mass planting is a sight to remember. The sturdy clumps can screen undesirable views or define intimate spaces. They also add rich, long-lasting fall color and winter interest to perennial borders. The unimproved species is an excellent garden plant; the named cultivars listed below are superb. All are good in Zones 5–9 unless otherwise noted and can be grown as described below.

How to Grow
Full or part sun. Ordinary or unimproved soil. Cut down to the ground in early spring. May spread, but is easily controlled. May self-sow. Propagate established clumps by division. Thrives in coastal conditions.

'Cloud Nine' is a medium-tall cultivar (4–6 ft.) with gray-green foliage that makes a beautiful foil for yellow coneflowers (*Ratibida* species), yellow-flowered cup plant *(Silphium perfoliatum)*, and other silphiums. Or plant a meadow patch with annual sunflowers, especially the branching types. (See photo on p. 162.)

'Haense Herms', sometimes called red switch grass, comes into its own in fall, with intense orange-red foliage in early to midautumn, deepening to plum purple as the season progresses. Its abundant flowers are also suffused with red tones. This grass has a looser, more weeping habit than other cultivars, growing as wide (3–4 ft.) as it is tall. (See photo on p. 163.)

'Heavy Metal' grows in a straight stunning column (3–5 ft.) of metallic blue foliage that contrasts wonderfully in the border with the colors and softer shapes of most perennials and annuals. Its good yellow fall color is almost a bonus. Like other switch grasses, this one maintains its form in the winter garden, when the stiff leaves bleach to tan. Try a clump or three with a drift of pink beebalm (*Monarda* spp.) and a sprawling mat of soft pink primrose *(Oenothera speciosa)*. Or go for bold and plant 'Heavy Metal' with other shouters like hot orange nasturtiums and orange-red Mexican sunflower *(Tithonia rotundifolia)*. Zones 4–9. (See photo on p. 163.) Another good cultivar with stiffly upright form is tall switch-grass, *P. virgatum* 'Strictum'.

'Rotstrahlbusch' ('Red Rays') tops many lists as the best red cultivar. It grows to 4 ft., and the foliage intensifies to a bur-nished red in midsummer to early autumn. Send shock waves through your garden by combining it with strong pink fall asters, or cool things off by planting with a foamy bed of blue mistflower *(Eupatorium coelestinum)*. (See photo on p. 164.)

'Squaw' is a 3–4 ft. clump like a fountain spilling from the center in all directions, turning purple-red by late summer. (See photo on p. 164.) 'Warrior' has a similar punch. Both cultivars are gorgeous with the bright orange, red, and yel-low fall foliage of deciduous trees and shrubs. The silvery plumes of early-blooming miscanthus cultivars, such as 'Flamingo', also make a strong partner, or try planting with cool-season grasses such as *Koeleria* — their tan dormant fo-liage will play up the deep tones of the red switch grasses. Another red-leaved cultivar, *P. virgatum* 'Rehbraun' ('Red-Brown'), has a muddier hue.

Pennisetum

pen-nih-see´tum
Gramineae. Grass family

Annual or perennial grasses with flat leaves and narrow, dense, fuzzy flower spikes that spray outward, giving the genus the common name "fountain grass." All are ornamen-tal in mixed beds, rock gardens, and with other grasses, and they thrive in containers. The flowers are also pretty in arrangements.

About 80 species, most native to tropical or warm cli-mates. Some grasses in this genus, generally the wider-leaved, late-blooming cultivars, such as 'Moundry' and 'National Ar-boretum', have become pesky weeds in parts of the country, especially California. If you live in a mild climate, check with your county extension office or the closest branch of the Na-ture Conservancy for advice on fountain grasses to avoid. Many experts are recommending Californians pass on the genus altogether.

■ *alopecuroides* (*see below for photos*)
(*P. japonicum*)
Fountain grass, Chinese pennisetum, Australian fountain grass
Zones 5–9. P/Cl/W
Height: 3–4 ft. Spread: 3–4 ft.

This warm-season perennial grass offers three-season interest. It makes a vibrant, flowing fountain of fine-textured leaves, dark green in summer and warm apricot, almond, or orange in fall, gradually bleaching to pale tan. It flowers freely from midsummer to midfall, with stems of fluffy foxtaillike spikes spilling outward like a fountain. Flowers may shade from reddish purple to coppery tan. An excellent plant to combine with spring bulbs — its fresh spring growth complements the bulb flowers, and it soon grows to cover the yellowing bulb leaves. It's also good as a ground cover or transitional plant bridging natural and more formal areas. The lovely arching form is mirrored in ponds and has a softening effect on rock or paving. A number of cultivars are on the market, including three diminutive fountain grasses.

'Cassian' is a free-flowering cultivar with outstanding fall color — it turns a rich golden yellow. The plant is dwarf, but the flowering stems can reach 2 ft. long, creating a luxuriant spray of soft spikes. Put it near the front of the border for close-up admiration. (See photo on p. 165.)

'Hameln' is another downsized version. It has very fine foliage and shorter flowering spikes and flower heads that are just the right fit for the mixed border. It blooms in early to midsummer. Zones 4–9.

The most diminutive of the small-scale cultivars, 'Little Bunny' grows in a petite tuft of leaves (6–12 in. round) and carries short, fluffy flower heads. Good for rock gardens or on a slope with soapwort and other mat-forming or small perennials. The little flowers are charming in fresh and dried arrangements. Zones 6–8.

A magnified version of the species, 'Japonicum' is the largest fountain grass cultivar, at 4–5 ft. tall and 4 ft. wide and bearing huge panicles of misty flowers. It is beautiful near water. Fine yellow fall color. Zones 6–8.

Two unusual fountain grasses, black-flowering 'Moudry' (see photo on p. 165) and the improved version, 'National Arboretum', are invasive grasses in warm climates. They seed themselves with a free hand and can escape from the garden into the lawn or the surrounding wild landscape. To lessen the risk of self-sowing, clip off flower spikes after enjoying them for a few weeks in the garden. They bloom later than other fountain grasses, in late summer to early fall. The spikes are dark, glistening brown when they emerge, and fluff out into reddish purple at the tips, with darker hearts, as they mature. Flowering is inconsistent. Some years, the flowers are held well out from the foliage; other times, they may be hidden among the leaves. 'National Arboretum' puts on a good show every year.

How to Grow
Full sun in the North; part shade in hotter climates. Does best in moist, well-drained soil, but tolerates other sites, too. Grows in acidic or alkaline soils. Tolerates dry spells, but the leaves get pale and curl up. Cut back old foliage in early spring, especially if planted with bulbs. Can be (but doesn't need to be) divided every five to six years. The center of the clump may die out, but that gap is noticeable only in early spring and doesn't matter later. Voles and mice may feed on the crown in winter. May be inexplicably short-lived, lasting only a few years in the garden. May self-sow. Grow from seed or propagate by division.

■ *macrostachyum* 'Burgundy Giant'   *p. 166*
Zones 9–10. P/Cl/W
Height: 4–5 ft. Spread: 4–5 ft.

A tropical grass from southern India with wider leaves and a less fountainlike habit than *P. alopecuroides*. Only the cultivar 'Burgundy Giant', a red-leaved plant, is commonly grown. Although it is very tender and will be killed at the first touch of freezing temperatures, it's so fast-growing that you can enjoy it as an annual in cold-winter climates. It has wide, strappy leaves up to an inch across and stout, upright stems. In midsummer long flower spikes, up to a foot long, arch above the wide column of foliage on erect stems, nodding like the foxtail grasses along roadsides.

The rich maroon foliage of this grass invites combinations with many other grasses, shrubs, and perennials. Hot red, orange-red, and yellow flowers like dahlias, Klondike cosmos, black-eyed Susans, and daylilies create a dramatic effect. Try it with pale pink and white flowers like nicotiana, geraniums, cosmos, and petunias, for subtle beauty. Leaves and flowers are outstanding in fresh arrangements.

How to Grow
Sun. Moist but well-drained soil. The flags of leaves will rip and shred in strong winds; plant it in a protected site. Water regularly if rain is scarce. Cut back in early spring. Propagate by division. You can also try propagating by stem cuttings rooted in sand and planted out the following spring.

■ *orientale p. 166*
Oriental fountain grass
Zones 7–9. P/Cl/W
Height: 1–2 ft. Spread: 1–2 ft.
This beautiful perennial grass forms gray-green clumps of arching foliage topped with equally arching spikes of pinkish purple flowers. It starts flowering two to three weeks earlier than *P. alopecuroides,* in midspring in mild-winter climates, and late spring to early summer in northern climates, where it is grown as an annual. The flowers last a long time, finally disintegrating by fall. Like other fountain grasses, the foliage mellows to golden tan and lasts all winter.

How to Grow
Sun to part or light shade. Well-drained soil. Thrives in sandy soils. Lighten heavy clay soils with generous helpings of compost, leaf mold, or aged manure. May self-sow. Propagate by seed or division.

■ *setaceum*
Tender fountain grass, crimson fountain grass
Zones 8–9. P/Cl/W
Height: 2–3 ft. Spread: 2–3 ft.
Tender perennial grown as an annual north of Zone 8. Makes an arching or mounded clump of fine-textured rusty green foliage. The fluffy, nodding spikes of rose or purple flowers, which can reach 12 in. long, are held well above the foliage from June through fall. Effective as a specimen or massed. Nice with pink-flowering nicotiana, which accents the pink tints of the grass flowers. This species self-sows and has become a weed in warm areas, such as California, where it is listed as one of the invasive exotics most difficult to control. The species *Pennisetum clandestinum,* Kikuyu grass, is also classified as a noxious weed there.

How to Grow

Full or part sun. Ordinary or unimproved soil. Somewhat drought-tolerant. When grown as an annual, it may need staking, especially in windy areas. As a perennial, cut foliage down in fall or spring. Self-sows and can be a weedy pest.

■ *setaceum* 'Rubrum' *p. 167*
(*P. setaceum* 'Atropurpureum'; also 'Purpureum', 'Atrosanguineum', and 'Cupreum')
Tender purple fountain grass, crimson fountain grass
Zones 9–10. P/Cl/W
Height: 3–4 ft. Spread: 2–3 ft.

This tender cultivar can be enjoyed as an annual in colder climates thanks to its fast growth and long season of flowering. The eye-catching burgundy foliage makes a good contrast in flower beds and is striking in large containers. It also makes a stunning mass planting, especially if silver-leaved artemisias are planted in front to emphasize the deep color of the grass. The long, arching flowers, which can be up to a foot long, are purple-red when they emerge, then mature to softer reddish purple and finally to brownish tan. The plant turns soft tan with a freeze.

'Rubrum Dwarf' is a downsized version, under 2 ft. tall, an excellent size for perennial gardens and containers. The foliage is ruddy and the arching flowers have a rich crimson hue. Try it in front of climbing pink roses like 'New Dawn', or old shrub roses like 'Koenigin von Danemark', where its fountain of leaves will mirror the arching form of the rose and its deep color will make the pale roses glow.

How to Grow

Sun. Well-drained soil; will thrive in clay and sandy, rocky, or loam soils. Good for coastal gardens. Propagate by division.

■ *villosum* *p. 167*
(*P. longistylum*)
Feathertop, tender white-flowered fountain grass
Zones 8–9. P/Cl/W
Height: 24–30 in. Spread: 18–24 in.

Valued for fluffy white plumes that look like elongated bunny tails, this tender perennial grass can be grown as an annual in cold-winter climates. It blooms from July through September. Best combined with flowering annuals or perennials that can cover the irregular mound of foliage — which isn't particularly attractive — and help support the flower stalks during rains or stormy weather. It's also an attention-getter when combined with dark-flowered 'Moudry' fountain grass.

How to Grow

Full or part sun. Ordinary soil; also thrives in sand. Propagate by seed. Good for coastal gardens. Not seriously weedy, but it has escaped in areas from Michigan to Texas. Doesn't last into winter; cut to the ground in fall.

Phalaris

fa-lay´ris
Gramineae. Grass family

Annual or perennial grasses, most with spreading rhizomes and thick, densely packed, pointed inflorescences. About 15 species from the north temperate zone, some of which are used as food for cage birds, as cotton sizing, and hay for livestock.

■ *arundinacea* 'Picta'   *p. 168*
(P. arundinacea var. *picta)*
Ribbon grass, gardener's garters
Zones 4–9. P/R/W
Height: 2–4 ft. Spread: 2–4 ft. or more

One of the first grasses grown as an ornamental, this plant is noted for its variegated foliage and fortitude. The upright stems hold green-and-white-striped leaves 4–10 in. long. One clump can lighten a dark-colored corner or provide a foil for clashing colors in a perennial border. The pinkish white flowers in midsummer are not particularly ornamental.

In all but very dry desert gardens, ribbon grass is a rampant grower, spreading by creeping roots. Choose a planting site carefully: once it's established, eradication is difficult because the grass springs up from any pieces of root left in the soil. You can control its spread by planting in a bottomless container or in defined areas such as parking lot islands. It makes a tough ground cover and the rhizomes are an effective soil stabilizer. It can also be grown as an aquatic, planted in shallow water a few inches deep or in a container surrounded by deep water.

'Dwarf Garters' is a more manageable cultivar. This shorty (12–15 in. tall) spreads more slowly than its taller relatives, but in the border you may want to confine it with barriers for peace of mind. It does best in part to light shade, not in sun.

'Feesey', also sold as 'Feasey's Form', is a fine-textured cultivar suffused with pink, especially in spring. The whitish flowers are showier than those of old-fashioned ribbon grass, but the plant spreads as aggressively. Best used in masses or along water. To emphasize the pink tints of the fresh foliage, plant with spring-blooming perennials in soft pink shades, such as hardy geraniums, soapwort, and rockcress. 'Feesey' tolerates some shade; grow in part shade in hot summer climates. (See photo on p. 168.)

How to Grow

Full or part sun. Not fussy about soil: tolerates sand or clay, acidic or alkaline conditions, wet or dry sites, some sea salt, and standing water. In most areas, the foliage is pretty in spring and early summer but turns brown by late summer. Cut it back to 6 in. and it will sprout fresh new growth. Easily propagated by division.

Phormium

for'mee-um
Agavaceae. Agave family
   Large clumping plants with spearlike leaves. Fibers from the leaves are woven into fishing nets and fabrics. Only two species, native to New Zealand.

■ *tenax* *p. 169*
New Zealand flax
Zones 8–10. P/Cl
Height: 8–9 ft. Spread: 8–9 ft.
   This plant has the same architectural effect as a hefty grass. The sword-shaped leaves, up to 9 ft. long and 5 in. wide, grow in crowded clumps of irislike fans. Clusters of reddish brown trumpet-shaped flowers are borne on tall naked stalks in summer. Compact 3–5-ft. cultivars fit into smaller gardens and make bold punctuation marks in a flower border. Many cultivars are named for their gorgeous leaf color: purple-red 'Atropurpureum', deep purple-red 'Rubrum', or 'Bronze'. Variegated cultivars 'Maori Sunset', 'Maori Queen', and 'Sundowner', all have bronze leaves striped with red, pink, and creamy white. 'Yellow Wave' has cheerful yellow-striped green leaves.

How to Grow

Full or part sun. Ordinary, well-drained soil. Plant from containers and allow plenty of space — phormiums get big fast. Needs no care beyond the removal of dead or damaged leaves and old flower stalks. May freeze back in cold winters, but recovers in one season. Can be divided, but you'll need several helpers to tackle a large specimen.

Phyllostachys

fil-lo-stak´is
Gramineae. Grass family

A large and useful group of hardy bamboos. Some grow quite tall, and all spread to make thickets or groves. The young shoots are eaten as a vegetable, and mature culms (stems) are used for fishing rods, plant stakes, fences, and timber. About 60 species, native to China.

■ *aureosulcata* p. 169
Yellow groove bamboo
Zones 6–10. P/R
Height: 15–20 ft. Spread: 15–20 ft. or more

One of the hardiest running (grove-making) bamboos. The woody, upright culms are rich green with yellow grooves that run vertically from node to node. They grow up to $1\frac{1}{2}$ in. thick and are good for plant stakes and light fencing. The narrow lance-shaped leaves are papery thin and light green. If spread is curbed, these bamboos can be used as a screen or hedge.

How to Grow

Full or part sun. Ordinary soil and watering. Plant divisions in spring, container-grown plants anytime. Zone 5 gardeners can grow these species like herbaceous perennials. The culms may freeze to the ground, but the roots are hardy to −20°F if protected with a layer of snow or mulch. These bamboos spread by underground rhizomes and can send up new shoots 20–30 ft. into your neighbor's yard. Mowing the shoots with a lawnmower won't keep the plant from spreading. You need to dig a trench and install a concrete, metal, fiberglass, or heavy plastic curb 18–24 in. deep when you first plant the bamboo. Don't be fooled into thinking cold winters will keep the plants under control; new shoots will surface in spring far from the parent. Maintenance is simple. Remove the oldest, tattered culms at ground level. Thin culms to create a grove. Shear hedges as desired.

■ *nigra* p. 170
Black bamboo
Zones 7–10. P/R
Height: 10–25 ft. Spread: 15–25 ft. or more

This bamboo has shiny black culms up to 1 in. thick and narrow, dark green leaves. It strikes a deep note against brighter green foliage, and like other bamboos, adds grace to masonry walls or fences. A confined grove is lovely in a Japanese-style garden. If you don't want to let it run in your garden, plant it in a generous container; put the container on

your patio or wherever the smooth black stems can be admired at close range. Also grown as a houseplant.

How to Grow
Same as *P. aureosulcata.*

Poa

poe´uh
Gramineae. Grass family

This large genus includes many familiar lawn grasses, such as Kentucky blue grass. More than 250 species (some authorities say 500 species) of annuals and perennials are native to North America, Eurasia, and other temperate regions of the world. In America, they are valuable forage and pasture grasses. Grass enthusiasts have introduced a few species to the horticultural trade.

■ *compressa*
Australian blue grass
Zones 8–10. P/Cl/C
Height: 1–2 ft. Spread: 1–2 ft.

This cool-season perennial holds promise as an ornamental grass for warm climates. It grows in dense clumps that green up early, making it a good choice for covering a slope. Despite its name, it doesn't look blue. Rolled leaf blades hide the blue undersides but give the grass its fine texture. The flowers are airy panicles that quiver in the breeze and ripen to golden tan.

How to Grow
Sun. Widely adaptable to soil types, but does best in moist, well-drained soils. Drought-tolerant. Good for coastal conditions. Like other recently introduced grasses, the limits of this one aren't fully known. It may prove to be more cold-hardy and is worth the experiment if you need a tough, adaptable grass.

Rhynchelytrum

(Rhychelytrum)
rink-ee-ly´trum
Gramineae. Grass family
   Native to Africa, the natal grasses get their botanical name from their peculiar seeds: *rhynch* is Greek for beak; *elytrum,* scale. They are annuals and perennials with showy, fluffy panicles of flowers. Taxonomists disagree on how many grasses belong to the genus; some say as few as 14, while others assign about 40 to this group.

■ *repens* *p. 170*
(Tricholaena rosea; Tricholaena repens)
Natal grass, ruby grass
Zones 9–10. P/W
Height: 1–4 ft., usually about 1–2 ft. Spread: 1–2 ft.
   Natal grass is a short-lived perennial that creates a billowy cloud of soft pink flowers. Its showy flowers and long bloom time — from summer almost through fall — make it immensely decorative in the garden, but it is a rampant self-sower in warm areas and has become a pest in Florida. The name ruby grass comes from the color of the newly emerged flowers, which are tinged purple to pink-red. As they mature, they soften to pinkish or creamy tan. The soft flowers are an excellent contrast to the dramatic spikes of bronze or variegated New Zealand flax *(Phormium tenax)* either together in large containers or in the garden. Or you can back them with the dark foliage of purple smoke bush. The flowers are beautiful in fresh arrangements. Natal grass can be grown as an annual in cold climates. Neither running nor clumping, natal grass grows in single stalks like wheat.

How to Grow
Sun. Will grow in almost all soils, but needs good drainage. Good for coastal gardens. Self-sows. Easy to grow from seed, or propagate by division.

Saccharum

sah-kar´um
Gramineae family

Large, robust perennial grasses of the tropical Old World, this genus includes more than 12 species (as many as 37 if grasses classified as *Erianthus* are counted). The hard stems are jointed like cane or bamboo, and the leaf blades are wide, arching, and often tipped with dangerously sharp points. Sugarcane *(S. officinarum)*, which is sometimes grown as an ornamental, is a member of the genus. If you've ever bought a piece of the sweet stalk at the grocery store, you'll have an idea of the thickness of this plant's stout, jointed stems. Cultivars of sugarcane are being developed for their ornamental possibilities in warm gardens. Growers are selecting for various combinations of color in both cane and leaves.

■ *officinarum* 'Pele's Smoke'
Red sugarcane
Zones 9–10. P/Cl/W
Height: 10–15 ft. Spread: 10–12 ft.

This huge grass has striking foliage in rich deep maroon-purple that looks almost purple-black in some lights. It grows in an upright clump, arching near the top. The stems are thick and jointed, up to 3 in. in diameter, and are just as richly colored as the foliage. The leaves are wide and strappy with rough edges. Flowers are a rarity. Plant as a specimen or in a grouping with other grasses. It makes a good background plant for grasses with light-colored flowers, such as 'Flamingo' miscanthus.

How to Grow
Sun. Thrives in many soils, but needs moisture and good drainage. Grows incredibly fast; worth trying as an annual in colder climates. Be careful working around this plant; the leaf blades are sharp and have pointed tips. Propagate by rooting cuttings of mature canes in moist sand, or hack a piece off an established clump.

Sasa

sa´suh
Gramineae. Grass family

Low-growing, spreading bamboos with broad leaves. They rarely flower. About 25 species, native to eastern Asia.

■ *palmata*
(*S. paniculata*; *S. senanensis*)
Running bamboo
Zones 7–10. P/R
Height: 6 ft. or more. Spread: 6 ft. or more

A rampantly spreading bamboo with slender erect stems. Papery thin, bright green leaves are clustered at the tips of the stems and branches; they keep their good green color even in winter. Stems are often streaked with purple, an interesting effect up close. Underground runners spread fast. Use it to control erosion on hillsides or streambanks, or install 18-in.-deep barriers at planting time and use it for a quick tropical or Oriental effect.

How to Grow
Sun or shade. Spreads fast in rich, moist soil; not quite so fast in ordinary conditions, but don't be lulled into thinking you can control it. Curb with a deep metal, fiberglass, or concrete barrier at planting time. Propagate by division. Dig up sections of 5–6 stems in early spring. Try to keep soil around the roots, and replant quickly. Needs little care — just cut old or shabby stems to the ground in spring. Doesn't tolerate desert heat or drought. Worth a try in Zone 6. It may freeze to the ground but will recover.

■ *veitchii* p. 171
(*S. albomarginata*)
Running bamboo, silver-edge bamboo, kuma zasa
Zones 7–10. P/R
Height: 2–3 ft. Spread: 3 ft. or more

A striking ground cover for shade, with broad, papery, bright green leaves that turn creamy white around the edges in fall. The variegated effect lasts all winter. Leaves are clustered at the ends of the slender canes. Indispensable for Japanese gardens; use with liriope, azaleas, water-smoothed stones, and bamboo fences.

How to Grow
Like *S. palmata.*

Schizachyrium

sky-zack´ree-um
Gramineae. Grass family
Mostly perennial grasses with a bunching habit. Closely related to Andropogon. More than 90 species, mostly tropical.

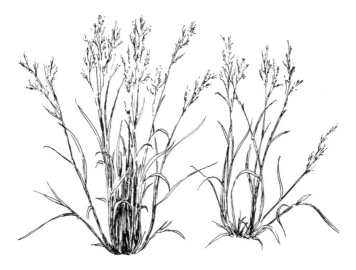

■ *scoparium* *p. 171*
(Andropogon scoparius)
Little bluestem
Zones 3–9. P/Cl/W
Height: 2–3 ft. Spread: 12–18 in.
A perennial warm-season native of the American tallgrass prairie, little bluestem is neither little nor blue. It forms erect clumps reaching knee-high or better (some plants may top 5 ft.) with slender green leaves that have a hint of blue near the base.

It's in the fall that this grass really shines, maturing to a burnished orange that is magnificent with the fall foliage of trees and shrubs. The color intensifies when the grass is wet after a rain. The summer flowers mature into fluffy seed heads that persist into winter. Borne along flexible stems that stand up even in a heavy snowfall, the small clusters of seed heads sparkle when backlit by the slanting rays of the sun. In the wintry landscape of bare dark branches, and especially against snow, this grass is unwavering as a flame.

Broomsedge *(Andropogon virginicus)*, often confused with little bluestem, has leafier stems, especially near the top, and less showy flowers: the small tufts are snuggled inside the bracts of the leafy stem instead of curling outward and downward like those of *Schizachyrium scoparius*. To make matters more confusing, it often hybridizes with little bluestem. Learning to tell the difference was once critical to land buyers because the presence of little bluestem indicated fertile soil good for growing wheat, while a lot of broomsedge meant that the land was overgrazed and the soil lean. In the landscape, though, broomsedge is just as appealing as little bluestem, with the same orange fall and winter color.

Little bluestem is an outstanding grass for the mixed border, where it mingles well with fall-blooming perennials such as short cultivars of purple New England asters. Its neat green tufts provide good structure in the summer garden, too. It can be used as a large-scale ground cover on dry sites, for erosion control, or as a transition between tended and natural areas. The seeds will attract native sparrows and other small birds. The fall foliage cut in bunches adds color and softness to dried arrangements of seeds and pods, or it can be twisted or braided into wreaths.

'The Blues', a bit taller than the species (up to 4 ft.), has gorgeous gray-blue foliage in tightly erect clumps that provide excellent vertical line in the garden. It is beautiful with pink astilbe, blue Russian sage, or other soft-textured perennials. Zones 4–9. The more compact cultivar, 'Blaze' (1–3 ft. high and 2–3 ft. wide), was selected for its excellent fall and winter color, which ranges from purplish orange to russet or reddish purple. It is commonly planted along highways in the Midwest and used to reclaim old strip mines in coal-mining areas.

How to Grow
Full or part sun. Ordinary or unimproved soil. Flourishes in hot weather, humidity, and dry soil. Thrives in sandy soil as well as clay. Shrugs off drought. Can self-sow, but usually doesn't. Propagate by dividing older clumps. When sowing large areas, use a water-filled lawn roller to push seeds well into soil. Cut back once a year, in early spring.

Schoenplectus

show-en-plek´tus

Cyperaceae. Sedge family

Annual or perennial grasslike plants that usually spread by creeping rhizomes. Stems may have the typical "edges" of the sedge family, three-angled to the touch, or they may be cylindrical. The stems form the "foliage" of these plants; true leaves are often absent altogether. About 80 species, found on almost every continent.

■ *lacustris* ssp. *tabernaemontani* 'Zebrinus'

(*S. tabernaemontana* 'Zebrinus'; *Scirpus lacustris* ssp. (or var.) *tabernaemontana* 'Zebrinus')

Zebra rush, banded bulrush

Zones 4–9. P/R

Height: 2–4 ft. Spread: 4 ft. or more

The erect, cylindrical "leaves" of zebra rush are spangled with horizontal yellow bands that look as if they've been splashed by dappled sunlight. Brownish flowers appear atop the speckled stems in summer and hang on into fall and winter, when the rush turns first yellow, then brown.

This bog plant is a good edge plant for ponds, where it will spread into the shallows, creating a graceful transition between land and water. Its porcupine-like foliage is a great contrast to the broad leaves and golden flowers of the western skunk cabbage *(Lysichiton americanus)*, a striking plant well known as an ornamental in Britain but not in its native America. Zebra rush also looks good with a spread of buttery yellow marsh marigolds *(Caltha palustris)* beside it.

How to Grow

Sun. Moist or wet soil or shallow water, to 1 ft. deep. Transplant young plants into the bog garden or at the pond edge in spring. Allow them room to spread, which they'll do at a moderately fast pace. Propagate by division, separating the rhizomes in spring.

Scirpus

skir´pus

Cyperaceae. Sedge family

Perennial grasslike plants that spread from rhizomatous roots. The erect stems are leafy, and flowers are borne in loose clusters at the top. About 100 species from around the world.

■ *cernuus*
(Scirpus filiformis; Isolepis gracilis; Isolepis cernua)
Low bulrush
Zones 8–10. P/Cl
Height: 6–12 in. Spread: 12–18 in.

The thin, hairlike stems and leaves of this interesting rush grow in a hummocky clump that looks like a mop-top Beatles wig. Tiny whitish conelike flowers dot the mound of foliage like a handful of fireflies or light-carrying fiber optics. (It is sometimes listed as "fiber optics grass.") Low bulrush is evergreen in Zone 10 and some parts of Zone 9; cut it back in other zones once foliage has gone dormant after frost. Plant this moisture-lover along the rocky edge of a garden pool, where it can spill prettily over the rocks.

How to Grow
Sun to light or part shade; if plant yellows, move to a shadier site. Moist to wet soil or very shallow water. Will also adapt to life in a container if you keep it well watered. Transplant a young plant to the garden in spring. Propagate by division in spring.

Semiarundinaria

sem-ee-uh-run-di-nay′ree-uh
Gramineae. Grass family

Running bamboos with woody culms that form tall, open thickets. They rarely flower. About 20 species, native to eastern Asia.

■ *murielae* p. 172
Running bamboo
Zones 7–10. P/R
Height: 10–15 ft. Spread: 10 ft. or more

This bamboo makes a tall, slow-spreading clump and isn't too invasive. Slender arching culms create a weeping-willow effect, but with denser foliage that makes a good screen.

How to Grow
Sun to moderate shade. Grows and spreads very slowly in unimproved soil. Gets taller and lusher in fertile soil amended with organic matter. Divide in very early spring, taking clumps of 3–5 stems with a good root ball, and replant promptly. Remove old or damaged stems. Trouble-free.

Sesleria

sez-lair´ee-uh
Gramineae. Grass family
More than 20 species of mostly perennial, usually small
grasses. Native to the moors and chalk highlands of Europe,
they are often called moor grasses.

■ *autumnalis* *p. 172*
Autumn moor grass
Zones 5–9. P/Cl/C
Height: 18 in. Spread: 18 in.
Moor grasses aren't particularly ornamental, but they are
undemanding and they offer evergreen foliage even in colder
climates. This species has perky yellow-green color that
brightens the shade under shrubs and trees, where you can
plant it in low-maintenance sweeps. Narrow spikes of flowers
push up in fall or in late spring in mild-winter areas.

How to Grow
Sun to light or part shade. Adapts to almost any soil. Tolerates drought. Thrives in coastal gardens and other difficult
sites. Propagate by dividing in spring.

■ *caerulea*
Blue moor grass
Zones 5–9. P/Cl/C
Height: 6–12 in. Spread: 6–12 in.
This perennial cool-season grass grows in a loose tussock
of lax narrow foliage. A silvery gray glint on one side of the
leaves gives the plant a bluish cast. The small spikes of
flowers are greenish at first and mature to pale whitish tan.
S. albicans, also called blue moor grass, is a very similar,
somewhat taller species with striking mauve flowers; the two
species are often confused.

How to Grow
Sun to part or light shade; plant in part or light shade in hot-
summer climates. Moisture-retentive soil. Propagate by division in spring or fall.

■ *heufleriana* *p. 173*
Green moor grass
Zones 5–9. P/Cl/C
Height: 12–18 in. Spread: 12–18 in.
The young leaves of this cool-season perennial grass are
powdered with white, giving the tuft a cool, frosty look. An-

other tough moor grass, this one is good in difficult conditions as well as in the sharp drainage of a rock garden.

How to Grow
Sun to part or light shade; part or light shade in hot-summer
areas. Drought-tolerant, but stays greener with more moisture. Propagate by division in spring or fall.

Sorghastrum

sor-gas´trum
Gramineae. Grass family
  Perennial grasses with narrow leaves, important chiefly as
fodder. More than 13 species, mostly from tropical regions of
Africa and the Americas.

■ *nutans* *p. 173*
(*S. avenaceum*; *Chrysopogon nutans*)
Indian grass
Zones 4–9. P/Cl/W
Height: 3–8 ft., usually 3–5 ft. Spread: 2 ft.
  Native to the tallgrass prairie, Indian grass forms tall narrow clumps that make a good vertical accent in the border
or massed as a background or screen. The slender leaves are
light green or blue in summer, bronze or burnt orange in fall,
and rich gold in winter. Slender downy flower heads are con-
spicuous for several weeks in late summer or fall. They open
golden and darken to bronze and can be used in fresh or
dried arrangements. A graceful grass that combines beautifully with Maximilian sunflower, purple coneflower, and
other native prairie flowers.

The abundantly flowering cultivar 'Holt' was developed with an eye toward practicality — as an improved forage grass for cattle — but it is beautiful in the garden or meadow. Planted in mass behind a similar mass of mid-height deep purple fall asters *(Aster novae-angliae)* it makes a stunning autumn combination.

How to Grow
Full or part sun. Can get floppy if the soil is too rich and moist, but stands up well if grown in lean, dry soil. Tolerates heat but appreciates an occasional watering during long dry spells. Propagate by seed or division. Cut back once a year, in spring. May self-sow, especially in undisturbed prairie or meadow plantings.

■ *nutans* 'Sioux Blue' *p. 174*
'Sioux Blue' Indian grass
Zones 4–9. P/Cl/W
Height: 3–5 ft. Spread: 2–3 ft.

This dramatic silvery blue cultivar stands very erect, providing an eye-catching vertical accent in a mass planting or as a specimen combined with red- or pink-flowered plants such as *Salvia coccinea*. It also makes an exclamation point next to sprawling gray-leaved plants like artemisias and helichrysum. Turns golden tan with orange highlights in fall.

How to Grow
Same as *S. nutans*.

Spartina

spar-teen´uh
Gramineae. Grass family
Perennial grasses that spread by rhizomatous roots, this genus is known as cord grass because the strong leaves of some species were once used to make cordage. About 15 species, native to Europe, Africa, America, and some islands.

■ *pectinata* *p. 174*
Prairie cord grass
Zones 4–9. P/R/W
Height: 4–6 ft. Spread: 6 ft. or more

Once found in marshy areas and lowlands from the Midwest to the East, this warm-season running grass of the American prairies has narrow arching leaves, spilling over in a fountain of greenery that turns golden tan in fall and winter. It is a determined spreader, so give it plenty of room to roam, and plant well away from passersby and children's play areas; its dangerously sharp-edged leaves can slice a finger in an instant. With these precautions in mind, this grass is a lovely choice to naturalize in a wet area or at water's edge. The narrow, shining inflorescences are pretty in a vase, either fresh or dried.

How to Grow
Sun to part shade. Moist or wet soil; will also grow in dry soils and is much more restrained in height and spreading habit there. Wear leather gloves and a sturdy long-sleeved shirt or jacket when working around this plant. Cut back in early spring, or simply let new foliage push up through old in naturalized plantings. Propagate by division any time during the growing season; cut back foliage first to make it an easier and safer job.

Spodiopogon

spoe-dee-oh-poe´gon
Gramineae. Grass family
A small genus of about nine species, almost all perennial. Only one of these is commonly grown as an ornamental. Native to both temperate and tropical regions of Asia.

■ *sibiricus* *p. 175*
(Muhlenbergia alpestris)
Frost grass
Zones 5–9. P/Cl/W
Height: 2–3 ft. Spread: 2–3 ft. or more
This clumping, warm-season perennial grass is often grown for its open panicles that bloom in late summer and fall, but the foliage habit is just as ornamental. The leaves jut out horizontally from the stems, giving it a look more like bamboo than grass. It spreads at a slow to moderate rate by rhizomatous roots.

Whether you use it singly, in a group, or in masses, frost grass carries plenty of weight in the garden, especially in fall. Its foliage becomes brown with streaks and tints of deep purplish red. Take advantage of its fall color by planting it with late-season perennials such as asters and sedum 'Autumn Joy', or situate it in front of mugo pine or other evergreens to show off the airy flowers. The flowers and foliage are attention-getters in fresh arrangements, especially when combined with pale pink chrysanthemums.

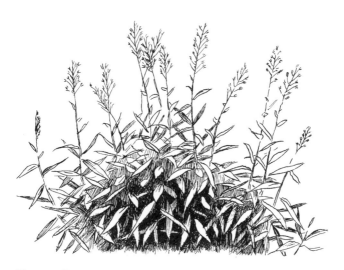

How to Grow

Light or part shade; sun in cool climates. It will also grow in deeper shade, but stake to keep it erect. Plant in moist but well-drained soil. Does best with regular watering or rainfall. Foliage becomes tattered in winter; cut back to ground in late fall. Propagate by division or seed in spring.

Sporobolus

spo-ro´bo-lus
Gramineae. Grass family

Annual or perennial grasses, usually clump-forming and fine-textured. Ripe seeds drop out of their hulls, giving these grasses the common name dropseed. About 100 species, native to the Old and New Worlds.

■ *heterolepis* *p. 175*
Prairie dropseed, northern dropseed
Zones 4–8. P/Cl/W
Height: 18–30 in. Spread: 18–24 in.

An excellent plant to start with if you are new to ornamental grasses. It forms an upright arching mound of fine, long leaves, emerald green in summer, turning gold with orange tints in fall. The color is stunning in winter. Panicles of small, delicate flowers are held 2–3 ft. above the foliage in late summer. The flowers have a unique fragrance — some compare it to buttered popcorn, others to coriander or melted wax. Pick them fresh for an intriguing touch in arrangements. Prairie dropseed can be grown as an accent plant, included in foundation plantings or mixed borders, or massed as a ground cover. A good transition plant between manicured gardens and natural areas. Native to moist prairies, it thrives in dry sites too.

How to Grow
Prefers full sun but tolerates part shade. Thrives with ordinary soil and watering, but tolerates dry, rocky soil. Cut back or mow in spring so seeds can fall, or propagate by dividing older plants.

Stipa
sty´puh
Gramineae. Grass family
   Mostly perennial grasses with slender, rough leaves and usually narrow panicles of flowers, sometimes with very long hairlike awns that give the inflorescences a silken sheen. The genus is dubbed needle grass because of sharp-pointed seeds. About 300 species, widespread around the globe in temperate and warmer regions. Recently reclassified, these grasses are now mostly assigned to the genus *Nassella*.
   Stipa grasses make excellent specimens in the mixed border or among other grasses. The flowers have a see-through effect above the large dense clumps of foliage. Translucent outer coverings remain after the seeds fall, giving a gentle, flaglike appearance to the grass for many weeks.

■ *cernua*
Nodding feather grass
Zones 8–9. P/Cl/C
Height: 1–2 ft. Spread: 1–2 ft.
   This delicate perennial grass is a western native. No longer widespread, it can still be seen along the roadsides in the foothills of the Sierra Nevada and California coastal range. The breathtaking flowers, which bloom in mid- to late summer, are held high above the foliage. Like similar American natives feather grass *(Stipa comata)* and purple needlegrass *(S. pulchra)*, *S. cernua* has long hairlike awns that glisten in the light like golden threads. Plant in groups for a stunning effect in a sunlit garden.

How to Grow
Full sun. Well-drained soil; thrives in sandy and rocky sites as well as in average garden soil and in clay. Drought-tolerant thanks to roots that can reach 15 ft. deep. With additional water, the clumps become more dense. Cut back after

inflorescences shatter. Stipa species can be tricky to cultivate. They seem to do best where they crop up naturally, in the American West. Grow from seed, or buy young nursery-grown plants. They require several seasons to become dominant; for the first year or two they remain tiny seedlings and need weeding. Once established, a clump may live 200 years.

■ *gigantea* p. 176
Giant feather grass
Zones 7–9. P/Cl/C
Height: 2–3 ft. Spread: 3–5 ft.

A cool-season perennial native to Spain, Portugal, and Africa, this fine-textured giant gets its name from its towering panicles of flowers. They stretch up to 4 ft. above the foliage and spread out in a wide sheaf up to 6 ft. across. The show is spectacular, with open, arching panicles of dangling flowers. Each seed is tipped by a long awn that shimmers in sunlight and shivers in the breeze. The grass blooms in late spring to early summer.

How to Grow

Sun. Well-drained, rich soil. Water regularly until the plant is well established. Can be tricky to propagate; it fails to thrive after dividing. Buy young plants and transplant in spring, or plant seed and be patient; it can take months to germinate.

■ *ramosissima* 'Pillar of Smoke'
Pillar of smoke
Zones 9–10. P/Cl/C
Height: 6–7 ft. Spread: 3 ft.

One of the newest introductions to American ornamental grasses, this cool-season Australian species grows in a tall, arching clump of fine leaves that emerge from a stand of bamboolike stems. The flowers start blooming in late winter and don't quit until the end of summer. They are finely textured panicles that arch out through the leaves along the entire sheaf of foliage, like wisps of smoke rising from a chimney. This plant has enough stature to work as a specimen, and it is dramatic in groups. A dark background makes the smoky effect outstanding.

How to Grow

Sun. Moist but well-drained soil; adapts to sandy and rocky sites as well as average garden soil. Cut back in fall. The plant's limits of cold tolerance aren't yet known; it may be hardy in Zone 8 or even colder areas. In California, it shows signs of becoming an invasive weed, having escaped from residential plantings to roadsides.

■ *tenuissima* *(see below for photo)*
Mexican feather grass
Zones 7–10. P/Cl/C
Height: 12–18 in. Spread: 12–18 in.

Mexican feather grass has a denser, more fluid look than the open California species. Clumps of extremely fine foliage spray upward and outward. The flowers appear above the foliage in a silky stream, emerging green in late spring to early summer, soon changing to a beautiful yellow-green, then finally to gold. The feathery inflorescences last well into fall and add softness to the garden and indoor arrangements. The cultivar 'Pony Tails' (see photo on p. 176) has abundant and very showy flowers that arch like a horse's silky, flaxen tail. Like other exotic stipas, it may hold the potential for becoming a troublesome weed.

How to Grow
Sun to part shade. Widely adaptable; needs good drainage. Will thrive in lean, sandy, or rocky soils as well as in the garden. Plant seeds or buy young plants and transplant to the garden in spring. Like other stipas, Mexican feather grass resents dividing. It self-sows abundantly, so plant it in a naturalized meadow or other setting where seedlings aren't a problem.

Tridens
try´denz
Gramineae. Grass family

Perennial grasses that grow in tufts or clumps. Flowers vary from tall delicate panicles to fluffy short tufts. Some 18 species, nearly all native to the Americas. Many are common roadside and field grasses.

■ *flavus*
Purple top
Zones 5–10. P/Cl/W
Height: 12–18. Spread: 18–24 in.

This warm-season perennial grows in fairly short clumps of slender foliage that are pleasant enough but nothing special, until deep burgundy flowers arise in late summer. The tall bare-stemmed panicles, so slight that they are barely noticeable close up, are beautiful when seen in a group from a distance, or set off against a light-colored masonry wall. The stems are dark, too, and the inflorescences are shiny. A common wild grass in the lower Midwest, it stretches for miles along unmowed roadsides like a plum-colored pool. The plant is valuable for fall and winter color, too, maturing to a warm golden tan and holding up the airy panicles through the winter. Plant in groups or masses or let it self-sow throughout a meadow garden; it's beautiful with native pale blue asters. Pick the fresh purple flowers for an airy touch in arrangements.

How to Grow

Full sun to moderate shade. Average garden soil. Also thrives in heavy clay and lean soils. Tolerates drought. Cut back old foliage in early spring. Self-sows moderately to generously. Propagate by seed or divide in early spring.

Tripsicum

trip´suh-kum
Gramineae. Grass family

Robust perennials with dense, flat leaves. Valuable as forage grasses in the Americas, they were also cultivated for grain by Central American Indians, who selectively bred *Tripsacum dactyloides* for an improved harvest. It was once thought that *Tripsacum* grasses may have been the ancestor of corn, but today that theory has lost ground because of an apparent lack of genetic compatibility — even when *Tripsacum* grows next to corn, the two don't hybridize. At least five species, native to the Americas.

■ *dactyloides* *p. 177*
Gama grass, gamma grass
Zones 4–9. P/Cl/W
Height: 6–10 ft. Spread: 6 ft.

The coarse, arching foliage of perennial gama grass grows in a large, often sprawling clump. The unusual flowers are slender, fingerlike spikes that arch over the foliage, accounting for the Greek name *dactyloides,* which means finger. Male and female flowers are separate, a trait unusual to most grasses but found also in the grass we know as corn *(Zea mays).* Both the orange stamens of the male flower, held above the females, and the purple stigmas of the female are highly noticeable in bloom. This is a big grass that thrives near water. Best in groups. Adds interesting texture and height to a shade garden.

How to Grow

Full sun to moderate shade. Moist soil, bog gardens, edges of ponds and streams. In the wild usually found in pure stands, unmixed with other plants; it will also naturalize in the garden. Leaf edges are rough and can cut; use care when working around them. Cut back after frost kills the foliage. Propagate by seed or division in spring. May self-sow.

Typha

ty´fuh
Typhaceae. Cattail family
   These familiar rushlike plants of wet places have wide, grassy leaves and erect, velvety brown pokers of flowers — the typical cattail. Some 10 species, found around the globe.

■ *latifolia* *p. 177*
Cattail, reedmace
Zones 4–9. P/R
Height: 3–5 ft. Spread: 3 ft. or more
   A perennial that spreads by rhizomatous roots to form thick colonies at water's edge and in shallow water. It has wide, strappy leaves and brown cigar-shaped pokers. The spikes persist until seeds fluff out and fly away in fall and winter. Foliage turns golden tan then bleaches to beige in winter.
   Narrow-leaved cattail *(T. angustifolia)* has a more refined look than the common cattail *(T. latifolia),* with slim, flat leaves and slender brown spikes that are usually about $\frac{1}{2}$ in. wide. The spikes of both species are striking in fresh or dried arrangements, but spray with clear polyurethane to keep them from turning to fluff.

How to Grow
Highly invasive. Choose a spot with care; once established, cattails are very difficult, if not impossible, to remove. Grow in sun, in almost any soil as long as it's wet. Colonizes in wet soil and in shallow water of less than a foot or so deep. Propagate by dividing the spreading roots. Let new foliage push up through old; it will quickly overtake it. Muskrats are fond of cattail roots and shoots and may dine on your planting. They're fun to watch, and the plants soon recover.

■ *minima*
Dwarf Japanese cattail
Zones 4–9. P/R
Height: 1–2 ft. Spread: 2 ft. or more
   There's no other word for this cattail but cute. About half the height of the common pond plant, it spreads more slowly too. Its short spikes and narrow leaves are perfect for small pools and large tubs of mixed water plants. Charming in arrangements.

How to Grow

Full sun to part or light shade. Adaptable to most soils as long as they are wet. Flourishes in shallow water. Divide in early spring.

Uniola

u-nee-oh´luh.
Gramineae. Grass family.

Perennial grasses that spread by creeping rhizomes. Only four species, native to salt flats and sand dunes of North and Central America. Some species formerly classified in this genus have been moved to *Chasmanthium*.

■ *paniculata p. 178*
Sea oats
Zones 7–10. P/R/W
Height: 3–8 ft. Spread: 3 ft. or more

A beautiful native grass, sea oats once covered the coastal dunes from Virginia to Florida and eastern Texas into Mexico. Today, it's an endangered species in the Southeast because of overpicking, foot traffic, and habitat destruction. Supervised, protected plantings are increasing its tenuous hold in the region. Important as a dune stabilizer, the grass has creeping roots that cover large areas of ground and hold the sand together. Heavy, drooping panicles of seeds start green and ripen to mellow tan. The flat spikelets are very similiar to those of *Chasmanthium latifolium,* wild oats, a grass that makes a good substitute in noncoastal gardens for this graceful, sand-loving native.

How to Grow

Full sun. Must have sand or very sandy soil; only for coastal gardens. Spreads in appropriate conditions by creeping rhizomes. Let it naturalize and avoid fussing with it; the roots are sensitive to disturbance by foot traffic.

Vetiveria

vet-ih-ver´ee-uh
Gramineae. Grass family

Also called vetiver, this genus includes only two species, both of them native to Old World tropical regions.

■ *zizanioides* *p. 178*
(Vetiver zizanoides)
Vetiver
Zones 9–10. P/Cl/W
Height: 4–10 ft. Spread: 4–6 ft.

A large grass that grows in dense tufts of slender leaves. Erect, fluffy panicles of flowers emerge in late summer to early fall. The aromatic, rhizomatous roots yield an oil used in perfumes, and the roots themselves are woven into screens and mats in India. The fragrance of the grass is most pronounced when dampened by the frequent warm rains of these regions. The plant has escaped from cultivation in some areas of the subtropical United States. It can sometimes be found growing wild in Louisiana. The stems are bare near the bottom, so grow this as a background grass with shorter grasses or other tropical plants in front. It's also useful as a hedge or screen, staying evergreen in frost-free climates.

How to Grow
Sun to part shade. Very adaptable. In its native haunts, vetiver grows on riverbanks and in other wet places, but it also thrives in average garden soil and tolerates drought. Cut back frost-killed foliage. Propagate by dividing in early spring.

Yucca
yuk´uh
Agavaceae. Agave family

Woody perennials with short or medium-high trunks and fibrous swordlike leaves. Erect, branched stalks bear large, usually white flowers and woody or fleshy fruits. About 40 species, native to North America. These plants grow in emphatic spiky clumps.

■ *filamentosa* *p. 179*
Bear grass, Adam's needle
Zones 5–10. P/Cl
Height: 2–3 ft. Spread: 5–6 ft.

This southeastern native is the most commonly offered yucca. It spreads slowly to make a wide patch with many rosettes of sword-shaped foliage. The evergreen leaves have sharp tips and curly fibers along the edges. The tall stalks of white flowers are very showy in June. Gather the woody pods in fall for dried arrangements. Plants sold as *Y. filamentosa* may actually be *Y. flaccida* or *Y. smalliana*; it's hard to distinguish among them.

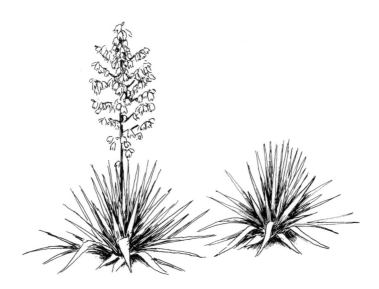

Yuccas aren't restricted to dry climates or xeriscape gardens. They combine well with perennials or grasses in a sunny bed or border. Individual clumps make a dramatic accent or focal point.

How to Grow
Full sun. Needs well-drained soil; thrives in poor, dry soil as well as average garden soil. Tolerates winter cold, summer heat, and wind. Transplant container-grown plants in spring. Established plants form offsets at the base that can be removed and transplanted. Only care required is the removal of old flower stalks and dead leaves.

Zea
zee´uh
Gramineae. Grass family
These Central American native grasses include only a few species (some authorities say two; others three or four), but their importance to humankind is immense. Maize has been a staple for thousands of years; "new" cultivars are still being developed from ancient grains found at archaeological sites. Male and female flowers are separate; the male flowers are in the tassel that tops the plant, the females in the inflorescences that form at leaf axils and mature into cobs of corn.

■ *mays* p. 000
Corn, maize
Zones 4–9. A/W
Height: 3–15 ft. Spread: 2 ft.

This annual grass is a food staple familiar to us as corn, but there are dozens of intriguing ornamental varieties that are worth a spot in the garden. The foliage of the plant has a strongly architectural quality and often striking leaf color. Try corn as a hedge or background planting.

Corn is easy to grow in any zone, though some varieties may not ripen their ears in short-season areas. Cultivars with unusual foliage are interesting garden plants in any area. Try 'Albovariegata', with white stripes on its green flags of leaves; 'Variegata', with stripes of creamy yellow or pinkish; 'Quadricolor', with fantastic foliage coloring of white, yellow, green, and pink. 'Red Stalker' has striking red and purple stalks; 'Harlequin' has beautiful deep red ears and leaves with red stripes. The many varieties of "Indian corn" also often show good red or purple coloring in their foliage; look for specialty heritage seed sources to find more unusual varieties with kernels in gleaming pink, steel blue, turquoise, deep red, and other hues.

How to Grow
Full sun. Rich, moist but well-drained soil. Plant seeds directly where they are to grow. Many gardeners look for young oak leaves as a sign that the time is right for planting. If you're planning to use the ears for decorative purposes, let them dry on the plant. Cultivars hybridize freely, since pollen is wind-carried. It's fun to try saving seed, or to try planting seed from an ear of ornamental corn that you've found elsewhere, but if you grow more than one kind of corn in your garden (or if there are neighboring farm fields), be aware that the seeds may not come true.

Appendices

Hardiness Zone Map

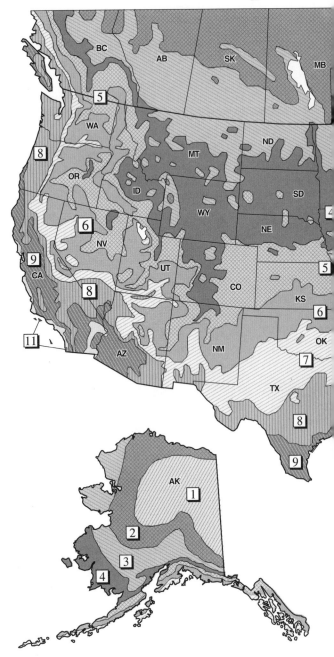

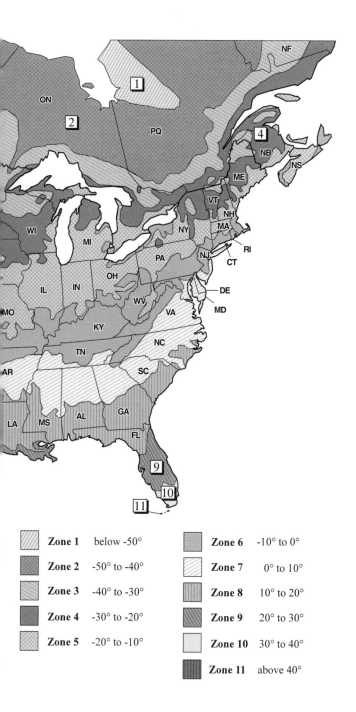

Zone 1 below -50°

Zone 2 -50° to -40°

Zone 3 -40° to -30°

Zone 4 -30° to -20°

Zone 5 -20° to -10°

Zone 6 -10° to 0°

Zone 7 0° to 10°

Zone 8 10° to 20°

Zone 9 20° to 30°

Zone 10 30° to 40°

Zone 11 above 40°

Sources of Seeds and Plants

Every year local nurseries offer a greater variety of ornamental grasses, but many of the grasses in this book will be available to you only through specialty mail-order suppliers like those listed below. You can order from them directly or through your local nursery. If you live nearby or are traveling in the area, be aware that some have demonstration gardens open to the public; phone to find out.

Kurt Bluemel, Inc.
2740 Greene Lane
Baldwin, MD 21013-9523
(410) 557-7229

Bluestem Prairie Nursery
13197 E. 13th Rd.
Hillsboro, IL 62049
(217) 532-6344

Carroll Gardens, Inc.
444 East Main St.
P.O. Box 310
Westminster, MD 21157
(800) 638-6334

Crownsville Nursery
P.O. Box 797
Crownsville, MD 21032
(410) 849-3143

The Flowery Branch Seed Company
P.O. Box 1330
Flowery Branch, GA 30542
(770) 536-8380

Greenlee Nursery
257 E. Franklin Ave.
Pomona, CA 91766
Fax only (909) 620-9283

Seeds Trust High Altitude Gardens
P.O. Box 1048
4150 Black Oak Dr.
Hailey, ID 83333
(208) 788-4363

Klehm Nursery
4210 N. Duncan Rd.
Champaign, IL 61821
(800) 553-3715

Limerock Ornamental Grasses, Inc.
70 Sawmill Rd.
Port Matilda, PA 16870
(814) 692-2272

Maryland Aquatic Nurseries
3427 N. Furnace Rd.
Jarrettsville, MD 21084
(410) 557-7615

Midwest Groundcovers
P.O. Box 748
St. Charles, IL 60174
(847) 742-1790

Milaeger's Gardens
4838 Douglas Ave.
Racine, WI 53402-2498
(800) 669-6956

Mostly Natives Nursery
P.O. Box 258
27235 Hwy. 1
Tomales, CA 94971
(707) 878-2009

Plants of the Southwest
Aqua Fria, Rt. 6, Box 11A
Santa Fe, NM 87501
(800) 788-7333

Prairie Moon Nursery
Rt. 3, Box 163
Winona, MN 55987
(Native grasses only)
(507) 452-1362

Prairie Nursery
P.O. Box 306
Westfield, WI 53964
(Native grasses)
(608) 296-3679

Shady Oaks Nursery
112 10th Ave. S.E.
Waseca, MN 56093
(507) 835-5033

Trans Pacific Nursery
16065 Oldsville Rd.
McMinnville, OR 97128
(503) 472-6215

White Flower Farm
P.O. Box 50
Litchfield, CT 06759-0050
(800) 503-9624

WHOLESALE ONLY
(Order through a local
nursery.)

**Native Sons Wholesale
Nursery, Inc.**
379 West El Campo Rd.
Arroyo Grande, CA 93420
(805) 481-5996

Sunny Border Nurseries, Inc.
1709 Kensington Rd.
P.O. Box 483
Kensington, CT 06037
(800) 732-1627

Photo Credits

Cathy Wilkinson Barash/Photo/Nats: 129A

C. Colston Burrell: 98–99, 126A, 128B, 130A

Priscilla Connell/Photo/Nats: 178A

Michael Dirr: 117B, 133B, 172A

Thomas Eltzroth: 72–73, 129B, 131A, 153A, 170B

Derek Fell: 46–47, 48–49, 52–53, 56–57, 68–69, 70–71, 74–75, 76–77, 78–79, 88–89, 90–91, 92–93, 94–95, 100–101, 106, 118A, B, 121A, 124B, 125B, 126B, 127A, B, 134A, B, 136A, B, 137B, 138B, 140A, 141B, 144A, B, 145A, 146A, B, 147B, 148A, B, 149B, 150A, B, 151A, 156B, 159A, B, 160B, 161A, 162B, 163A, B, 164A, B, 166A, 167B, 168B, 169B, 173B, 174A, 175B, 176B, 177A, B, 178B, 179B

Dency Kane: 58–59, 116A, 125A, 165A, 170A

Charles Mann: 50–51, 104–105, 110–111, 119A, B, 122B, 123A, B, 124A, 131B, 160A, 161B, 171B

Jerry Pavia: 54, 55, 60–61, 80, 81, 84–85, 86–87, 96–97, 102–103, 107, 108–109, 112–113, 120A, 122A, 139A, 142A, 145B, 156A, 158A, 165B, 167A, 169A

Ben Phillips/Photo/Nats: 133A, 147A, 152A, 178A

PhotoSynthesis: 82–83, 117A, 120B, 121B, 128A, 132A, B, 137A, 162A

Steven Still: 62–63, 64–65, 66–67, 130B, 135A, B, 138A, 139B, 140B, 141A, 142B, 143A, B, 149A, 151B, 152B, 153B, 154A, B, 155A, B, 157A, B, 158B, 166B, 168A, 171A, 172B, 173A, 174B, 175A, 176A, 179A

Index

Numbers in **boldface** *type refer to pages on which color plates appear*